Making Marvelous Wood Toys

Tim & Tom Lynn

Sterling Publishing Co., Inc.   New York

Toy designs by Tom and Tim Lynn

Drawings by Tim Lynn
Photography by Melissa West, Aloha Photography
Toy parts for picture on first page of color section from Meisel Hardware
Specialties and Cherry Tree Toys, Inc.

Library of Congress Cataloging-in-Publication Data

Lynn, Tim.
   Making marvelous wood toys/Tim & Tom Lynn.
      p. cm.
   Includes index.
   ISBN 0-8069-6744-7 (pbk.)
   1. Wooden toy making. I. Lynn, Tom. II. Title.
TT174.5.W6L96 1988   88-15947
745.592—dc19   CIP

          1   3   5   7   9   10   8   6   4   2

Copyright © 1988 by Tim & Tom Lynn
Published by Sterling Publishing Co., Inc.
Two Park Avenue, New York, N.Y. 10016
Distributed in Canada by Oak Tree Press Ltd.
c/o Canadian Manda Group, P.O. Box 920, Station U
Toronto, Ontario, Canada M8Z 5P9
Distributed in England by Cassell
Artillery House, Artillery Row, London SW1P 1RT, England
Distributed in Australia by Capricorn Ltd.
P.O. Box 665, Lane Cove, NSW 2066
Manufactured in the United States of America

Contents

Acknowledgments   *4*

1. The Basics of Toymaking   *5*
Toymaking Tips   *6*
Lumber   *8*
Tools   *11*
Clear Finishes   *19*
Toy Safety   *21*

Color Section follows page 32

2. Toys   *33*
Trojan Horse   *34*
Sewing Machine   *37*
Buzz Saw   *41*
Don Quixote   *45*
Cradle   *49*
Duck Pull Toy   *52*
Telephone   *55*
Rocking-Pig Bank   *58*
Camera   *63*

Toaster   *67*
Iron Set   *70*
Jalopy   *73*
Dump Truck   *76*
Big Horn Pull Toy   *80*
Gas Pump Bank   *84*
Robot   *91*
Big Train   *96*

3. Commercial Toymaking   *109*
Selling Toys   *110*
Production Tips   *115*

Appendices   *123*
Metric Equivalency
   Chart   *124*
Toy Safety   *125*
Copyrights   *126*
Key to Toy Parts   *127*

Index   *128*

ACKNOWLEDGMENTS

We want to thank the members of our family for their help, encouragement, inspiration and support.

Thanks to:

Ginger, for good advice, for hard work, and for typing the manuscript (and typing . . . and retyping).

Dad, for inspiring us to make toys by making beautiful wooden triplanes and log trucks for us when we were young. Mom, for nurturing our creativity by encouraging us to find things to do when we were kids (other than to watch TV).

Claudia, for unsplitting our infinitives.

Bill, for getting us started in woodworking and for contributing tools, ideas and good humor.

Eileen, for protecting book materials from kids with peanut butter.

Larry, for help with the toy business.

Uncle Jim, whose cartoons and art work inspired Tim to develop his own graphic art skills.

Aunt Een, for providing reference material and much-needed encouragement.

And finally, thanks to all the kids in our family for inspiring new toys and testing old ones: Solomon, Kyle, Wilson, Selina, Andy, Arune, Nahlee, Andrew, Jené, Amber, and Heather.

1
THE BASICS OF TOYMAKING

Toymaking Tips

Larry's stomach growled and his mouth watered in anticipation of his afternoon snack— one jumbo bag of crunchy corn chips. His mind had been filled with thoughts of these tasty morsels all day long. But now, when the time had come to enjoy them, he was unable to open the bag.

With increasing desperation and decreasing patience, he gripped the cellophane between his teeth and tried to gnaw his way through. The sight of the salty, crunchy chips so close to his mouth was enough to obscure his better judgment. Larry flung the bag of chips onto the drill-press table and lowered the twirling bit. The expected tidy hole did not appear. Instead, the machine yanked the bag from his hands and spun it around and around until centrifugal force exploded the cellophane with a mighty bang.

With his mouth open (and still watering), Larry watched as the chips spun through the air and landed, in a perfect circle, on the concrete floor.*

In this section we offer advice and tips to anyone interested in making wooden toys. Our first bit of advice? *Don't use the drill press to open a bag of corn chips.*

*This story is true. The names have been changed to protect the foolish.

Designing Wood Toys

There is nothing quite like the excitement and satisfaction that comes from building a toy you have designed yourself. Try it. You may find toy-designing the perfect outlet for creativity.

Many people think that artists and designers are born with the ability to visualize a creation in every detail before they begin to create. Don't worry if you don't have this ability; few (if any) do. Most finished works end up somewhat, if not vastly, different from what the artist originally had in mind. That's half the fun of designing. It doesn't take special talent to design wood toys. With practice, anyone can do it. All you need is to be willing to experiment and to learn to trust your artistic judgment.

GETTING AN IDEA

The first step in designing a toy is to come up with a good idea. One quick look around your own home will probably give you plenty of toy ideas. After all, toys are often child-sized versions of objects from the adult world, and the typical home is full of objects. In the kitchen there is a stove, a sink, and small appliances. In the garage there is a lawn mower, some wrenches, a car, a jack, a workbench, a broom and some power tools. Any one of these things could inspire a wonderful wood toy. Once you

begin to look, you will find yourself surrounded by an endless supply of toy ideas.

Mechanical or physical principles can also inspire toy ideas. Many of the classic folk toys must have started with someone's fascination over the way that an object behaved when a force was applied in a particular way. Think of the spinning top, the yo-yo, the climbing bear, or the whistle. Even as adults, with a basic understanding of the principles involved, we find these toys captivating. For a child, they are absolutely spellbinding.

Those toymakers who are mechanically minded will be inspired by the lever, the gear, the cam, the inclined plane, the spring, and the wheel. You will explore fully the possibilities of a rubber band and will be challenged to design toys powered by the wind, by gravity, or by water. For you, designing will be inventing.

Others may want to look to literature for toymaking ideas. We have included, in this book, a plan for a Don Quixote pull toy. You might want to design a toy inspired by *Moby Dick*, Mother Goose, or Noah's ark.

No matter what you use as a source of inspiration, an enthusiasm for the original idea will help to make the design and construction of your wooden toys an enjoyable experience.

DETERMINING DIMENSIONS

Once you have a good idea, you can decide upon the basic size of your toy. Keep in mind that, unlike the modelmaker, the toymaker has freedom to change dimensions for artistic reasons. For example, a car can be made to look sleek and sporty by exaggerating its length, or cute and funky by exaggerating its height. As a designer, the decision is yours. When determining dimensions, however, don't forget to take into account the dimensions of a child's

hands. There are limits to what small hands can grasp, pick up, push and pull.

EXPERIMENTING

At this point, some designers make sketches to help them to visualize their idea, while others prefer to skip to the next step and begin mocking-up crude variations of their toy from scrap wood. Either method will work. The important thing is that you consider many different possibilities before deciding upon the one that, in your judgment, is just right. Here are some things that you may wish to try while experimenting with your toy design:

——Change the relative proportions of some of the main parts. Try shortening the wingspan of an airplane, for example, while enlarging the pilot and propeller.

——Experiment with curved and straight lines, circles and angles. Lines and angles generally give a toy a harsher quality than the softness of curves and circles.

——Add and subtract detail. The temptation is usually to add too much detail to a toy. It is usually more desirable to carefully select a few details than to clutter a toy with too much embellishment. Keep it simple.

——Incorporate curves and cuts in your design which are compatible with your tools. If you have a bandsaw that will cut no smaller than a 2-inch radius, use a curve with a 2-inch or greater radius in your toy design.

Once you have experimented with your design and have made the preliminary artistic decisions, you will be ready to begin working on your masterpiece. But don't feel bound by any of the decisions you have made. If, along the way, you decide to deviate from your original plan, do it. After all, you are the designer.

Lumber

"Hardwoods—warehouses one through five. Softwoods—six and seven," mumbles the salesman. The sweeping gesture of his arm indicates a vague direction somewhere between Tierra Del Fuego and the prime meridian.

You find yourself wandering through huge warehouses packed to the rafters with lumber. What looks like birch is marked maple. What seems soft is called hard. What is labelled a foot—isn't. The approaching lift truck is a welcome sight.

"Wha'-da-ya-wan'?" bellows the driver.

"Well," you begin, "I need some hardwood to make a few toys, and I was wondering about the different . . ."

"Yeah, yeah," the driver interrupts, embarking on a monologue of Lumbo Jumbo. "We've-got-hundreds-of-species-from-Honduras-mahogany - to - cocobolo - in - eight - quarter - four-quarter-select-and-better-S1S-S2S-FAS-no-selection-take-it-from-the-top-and-leave-all-stacks-straight - flat - and - even - or - there's - a - blinkin'-blankety-restacking-charge." And with that pithy bit of information, the lift truck roars off in a haze of monoxide.

Although listed in the telephone directory under Retail/Wholesale, somehow you get the notion that this lumberyard is more interested in selling by the boxcar than by the board.

Many lumber outlets, however, actively compete for the business of craftsmen. Individual woodworkers buy only modest quantities of lumber, but their purchases collectively represent a sizable portion of total lumber sales.

Some of these stores prefer to deal primarily with the crafts market. In addition to lumber, they offer woodworking tools, finishes and project plans. Woods in these stores are surfaced and attractively displayed in well-lit showrooms. The salespeople are often experienced woodworkers themselves and are helpful in choosing wood and woodworking items for each project. Lumber-purchasing is obviously much more pleasurable in this type of store. A few quick phone calls will help to identify these outlets in advance.

No matter where you purchase toymaking wood, or how well-versed the salespeople are, there is no substitute for a firsthand knowledge of how wood is classified, measured and graded. With this in mind, we offer an introductory course.

Lumbo Jumbo 101

HARDWOODS AND SOFTWOODS

Woods are divided into two basic groups—hardwoods and softwoods. The assumption that hardwoods are hard and softwoods are soft

is a frequent misconception. Hardwoods come from trees that lose their leaves at the end of a growing season (deciduous). Softwoods are cut from cone-bearing trees (conifers). Even though balsa wood is lightweight and spongy, it is a hardwood.

MEASURING LUMBER

Lumber can be measured by the linear foot (lin. ft.) or by the board foot (bd. ft.). Dimensioned lumber is usually sold by the linear foot, which is a measurement of length only. A board foot is most often used when measuring hardwoods, and is a standard measure of quantity. Length, width, and thickness are used to calculate a measurement in board feet: A piece of wood 1 ft. long × 1 ft. wide × 1 in. thick contains 1 bd. ft. of lumber. To find how many board feet of lumber are in a particular board, multiply its dimensions in inches and divide by 144.

GRADING

Certain standards have been set to judge the quality of lumber. Both hardwoods and softwoods are evaluated for knots, cracks, and other defects. Hardwoods are further evaluated according to length and width. Each piece of lumber is then assigned a grade.

The better quality softwoods are termed "select" and are further distinguished from the best to the worst—A, B, C and D. The lower grades of softwood are called "common" and are numbered from the best (#1) to the worst (#5).

The best hardwood boards go into "firsts and seconds" (FAS). The lower hardwood grades are called "select" and "common."

DIMENSIONS

Standard lumber sizes refer to lumber before it has been dried and surfaced.

Softwood: In its rough form a 2 × 4 measures 2 inches thick × 4 inches wide. When you purchase it at the lumberyard, it has been dried and surfaced, reducing it to an actual measurement of 1½ inches × 3½ inches. The dimensions of other softwoods are similarly reduced.

Hardwood: Hardwoods are available in random lengths and widths and in a variety of thicknesses. The thickness of a hardwood board is usually expressed as a fraction. A board which measures 1 inch thick when rough is called "four quarter" (4/4). Hardwood can be purchased rough, surfaced on one side (S1S),

SOFTWOOD DIMENSIONS
(in inches)

Thickness		Width	
Standard Size (Rough)	Actual Size (Surfaced)	Standard Size (Rough)	Actual Size (Surfaced)
½	7/16	2	1½
1	¾	4	3½
2	1½	6	5½
4	3½	8	7¼
Lengths of softwood are available in two-foot intervals.		10	9¼
		12	11¼

9

surfaced on 2 sides (S2S), or surfaced on both sides and both edges (S2S, S2E). A four-quarter surfaced board will measure 13/16 in. thick. Likewise, an eight-quarter (8/4) board will measure 1¾ in. after surfacing. Some hardwood lumber dealers will also surface and cut boards to a customer's specifications.

Which Woods to Use

There are thousands of varieties of hardwood and softwood, and with the exception of a few (notably rosewood and cocobolo from the Dalbergia family, which can be allergenic), all can be used for making wooden toys. Most toymakers choose wood from a select group:

Softwood: pine, Douglas fir, cedar
Hardwood: (moderately priced) poplar, beech, maple, and birch
(more expensive) black walnut, red gum, and Honduras mahogany.

These woods are chosen not only because of their beauty, but because they can be cut, shaped, and sanded easily.

Light-colored softwoods make up the bulk of the woods used in toymaking. These woods are usually more available and less expensive. But it's not unusual to see toymakers mix bits of darker hardwood with softwood to give their toys added contrast and color. Used in this way, one board of expensive hardwood can go a long way.

By experimenting with different varieties of wood, you will become familiar with their unique characteristics and be able to make the right choice for each toy project.

Sources of Wood

If you have the inclination (and aren't bothered by a little legwork and a few phone calls) you can acquire wood for your toymaking projects quite cheaply. Since toymakers can use many of the small scraps of lumber that might otherwise be burned as firewood, it isn't always necessary to get lumber from the traditional sources (lumberyards, hardwood stores, and mail-order catalogues).

Lumber mills trim the ends of dimensioned lumber to make the boards uniform and to get rid of end cracks. Although these cutoffs are usually sold by the thousand board foot unit through lumber brokers, smaller mills will sometimes sell lesser amounts directly.

Cabinet shops and furniture manufacturers have trouble disposing of their scrap wood fast enough. For them, getting rid of these scraps is often a bothersome expense. Most are more than happy to have it hauled away.

Gun shops sometimes make their own gunstocks. Although these scraps are generally small and oddly shaped, the wood is often exquisitely beautiful, and is usually given away or sold inexpensively.

Warehouses and factories throw out old hardwood pallets and packing crates that can be dismantled and used for toymaking.

Tools

"Don't you ever use power tools?" asked one of the children who had gathered to watch Wilbur make wooden toys. The old man stroked his beard, puffed on his pipe, and in a slow drawl, answered, "Used to. Yep, had a whole shop of 'em, hummin', whistlin', and turnin'. Got rid of 'em after the accident." Wilbur replaced his pipe, lit it and went back to making toys.

Unable to contain herself for another second, a wide-eyed little girl blurted, "What accident?"

"Well," Wilbur continued, "must 'a been four years ago come spring. I was out cuttin' a piece of pine on the table saw, when it bound up. The back kick sent me a-reelin' and I fell on a stack of boards. Didn't hurt me much, though. The top board was pulled out a little, don't ya know? Kind of like sittin' on a teeter-totter. Blue didn't make out so well. He was sleepin' on the other end of that very same board. Vaulted him into the air just like a circus veteran. Prettiest triple flip. Poor Blue. You see, the middle of that dog's flight brought him right even with the dust collector tube. Sucked him up. From that day on, I vowed never to use another power tool."

"Did he die?" asked the little girl, fighting back her tears.

"Who?" responded Wilbur.

"Blue!"

"Oh, no! We were able to extricate him. Yep, he's fine. Considerin' all the greasin', tuggin' and pullin'. He's adaptin' well, too. Yep, good ol' Blue. Used to come curl up right at my feet . . . now he's gotta coil."

Like Wilbur, most woodworkers, at some point, develop a preference for certain types and designs of tools. Fortunately there are many alternatives. The basic toymaking operations of cutting, shaping and boring can be done with a variety of hand and power tools.

Toymaking is popular, in part, because it can be done with ordinary woodworking tools. A surprising number of toys can be made with just a crosscut saw, a coping saw, and a hand drill. But if you are like most people, you will soon find yourself drooling over mail-order tool catalogues and leaving wish lists conspicuously placed around the house.

If your dreams don't match your finances, you might consider purchasing secondhand tools and machinery. Many woodworkers find the quality of used items to be comparable to, if not better than, the quality of new ones. They prefer the heavy castings of older tools to the metal alloys and plastics used in the construction of newer versions.

Before purchasing a used machine or tool, however, you should inspect it carefully. Make sure the bearings are tight, that it operates prop-

erly, and that there are no pieces missing. Find out if the manufacturer is still in business. Ask yourself these questions:

——Are parts, blades and accessories available?

——Does the motor use single-phase (household) or 3-phase (industrial) power?

——Will my electrical system accommodate the motor amperage?

When acquiring tools for the workshop, don't overlook three of the most important—ear protectors, goggles, and a vapor mask.

Tool Index

HAND TOOLS

Crosscut Saw: The crosscut saw, with its closely spaced teeth, is designed for straight cutting across the wood grain (Illus. 1).

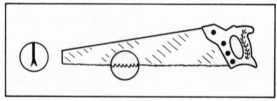

Illus. 1. Crosscut saw.

Ripsaw: The ripsaw has chisel-like teeth for making straight cuts in the direction of the wood grain (Illus. 2).

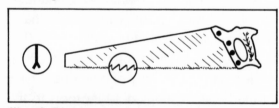

Illus. 2. Ripsaw.

Keyhole Saw: The keyhole saw, with its tapered blade, is designed for cutting inside curves and is perfect for starting cuts from slots and holes (Illus. 3).

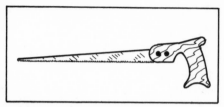

Illus. 3. Keyhole saw.

Coping Saw: The coping saw has a thin blade, which makes it a good tool to use for cutting inside and outside curves (Illus. 4).

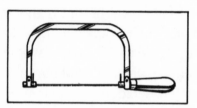

Illus. 4. Coping saw.

Backsaw: The backsaw is a fine-toothed saw with a braced back. It's used in conjunction with a mitre box to make precision angle cuts (Illus. 5).

Illus. 5. Backsaw.

HAND-HELD POWER TOOLS

Circular Saw: The circular saw is used for making straight cuts across or with the wood grain. The base is adjustable for making bevel cuts (Illus. 6).

Sabre Saw: The sabre saw is a hand-held jigsaw that is used to cut outside or inside curves (Illus. 7).

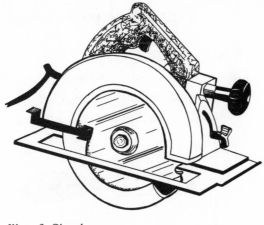

Illus. 6. Circular saw.

Illus. 8. Table saw.

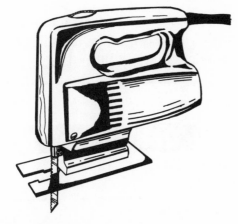

Illus. 7. Sabre saw.

STATIONARY POWER TOOLS

Table Saw: The table saw includes a mitre gauge for crosscuts and a guide fence for ripping lumber to specific dimensions. It is adaptable to many specialized jigs and accessories (Illus. 8).

Radial Arm Saw: The radial arm saw is a rotary pullover saw. It is primarily used for crosscutting, but it can also be used for ripping, mitring, and bevelling (Illus. 9).

Bandsaw: The bandsaw is used to make irregular cuts. Its table can be tilted to make bevel cuts. The bandsaw is among the most useful tools for the toymaker to own (Illus. 10).

Illus. 9. Radial arm saw.

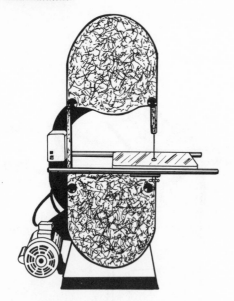

Illus. 10. Bandsaw.

Jigsaw: The jigsaw (or scrollsaw) has a thin blade which is powered in a reciprocating motion. It can be used to make intricate curves as well as inside cuts (Illus. 11).

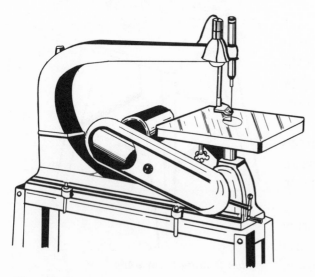

Illus. 11. Jigsaw.

For Shaping Wood

HAND TOOLS

Chisel: The chisel is a knife-like cutting tool with a sharp, bevelled edge (Illus. 12).

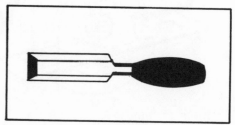

Illus. 12. Chisel.

Rasp: The wood rasp is a tool with coarse file teeth, which is used for rounding and shaping the edges of wood (Illus. 13).

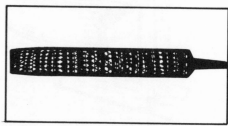

Illus. 13. Rasp.

Hand Sanding-Block: A hand sanding-block is a rubber sandpaper holder used to make hand-sanding easier (Illus. 14).

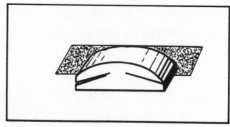

Illus. 14. Hand sanding block.

HAND-HELD POWER TOOLS

Router: The router is a high RPM machine which is generally used for cutting grooves and rounding edges. There are many shapes and styles of router bits available (Illus. 15).

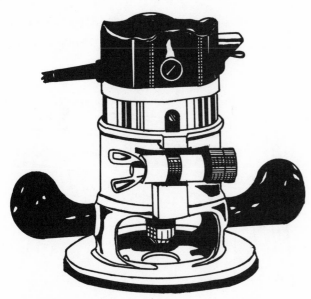

Illus. 15. Router.

Finish Sander: The finish sander is a hand-held tool which is used to vibrate an abrasive sheet in order to quickly smooth the surface of wood (Illus. 16).

Illus. 16. Finish sander.

Stationary Power Tools

Combination Sander: The combination sander consists of a disc sander and a belt sander. It is used to sand the surface and sides of boards.

Its abrasive sanding belts and discs are available in various grits. The disc sander and belt sander are also available as separate machines (Illus. 17).

Illus. 17. Combination sander.

Strip Sander: The strip sander uses a narrow abrasive belt. It is useful for sanding small toy parts and can also be used to sharpen tools (Illus. 18).

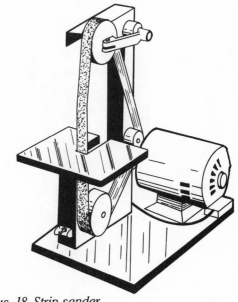

Illus. 18. Strip sander.

Jointer: A jointer is a rotary-knife machine used to prepare the edges or reduce the thickness of a board (Illus. 19).

Illus. 19. Jointer.

Planer: A planer is a rotary-knife machine used for smoothing the surface and reducing the thickness of lumber (Illus. 20).

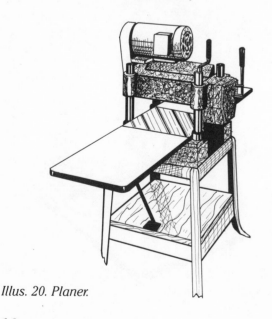

Illus. 20. Planer.

Lathe: The lathe rotates a piece of wood so that it can be shaped with various knife-like turning tools (Illus. 21).

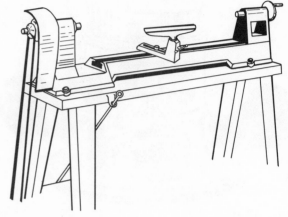

Illus. 21. Lathe.

For Boring Wood

HAND TOOLS

Brace: The brace is a device for holding and turning a bit and is used for boring medium to large diameter holes (Illus. 22).

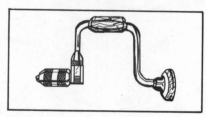

Illus. 22. Brace.

Hand Drill: The hand drill is a tool which is gear driven for faster bit rotation and is used for drilling small diameter holes (Illus. 23).

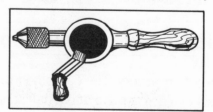

Illus. 23. Hand drill.

POWER TOOLS

Portable Electric Drill: The portable electric drill is a hand-held boring tool. The bench-drill stand, drill guide and dowel jig are accessories that can add to its versatility (Illus. 24).

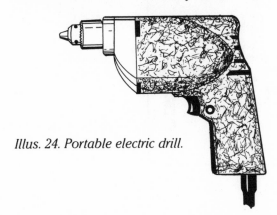

Illus. 24. Portable electric drill.

Drill Press: The drill press is a stationary power tool for drilling accurate perpendicular holes. It can be adjusted for drilling to a specific depth (Illus. 25).

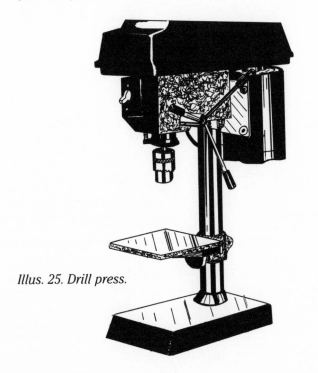

Illus. 25. Drill press.

Boring Accessories

Brad-point Bit: The sharp center point and side spurs of the brad-point bit aid in drilling clean-sided holes of small-to-medium diameter (Illus. 26).

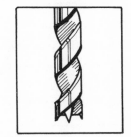

Illus. 26. Brad-point bit.

Multi-spur Bit: The multi-spur bit is used to bore clean, precisely located holes, and is available in medium-to-large diameters (Illus. 27).

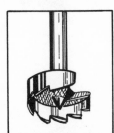

Illus. 27. Multi-spur bit.

Forstner Bit: The Forstner bit is a drill bit which drills shallow, flat-bottom holes (Illus. 28).

Illus. 28. Forstner bit.

Plug Cutter: Plug cutters are available in several styles and sizes and are used for cutting various diameter plugs and short lengths of dowel (Illus. 29).

Illus. 29. Plug cutter.

Circle Cutter: The circle cutter is a useful drill-press accessory for making holes and circles of various diameters (Illus. 31).

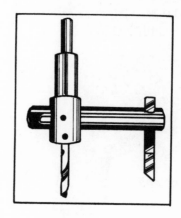

Illus. 31. Circle cutter.

Hole Saw: The hole saw is a cup-shaped cutter with saw teeth and a twist bit center. It is used for cutting holes and circles and is available in various sizes (Illus. 30).

Illus. 30. Hole saw.

Clear Finishes

BEN: Hello, Sylvia? This is Ben. Listen, I was about to put the finishing touches on a wooden log truck that I made for the kids, and I got to looking on the side of the finish can. It says, "Not for use on surfaces accessible to children." I was trying to figure what sort of clear finish to use, and Alice said to call and get your advice. We were wondering what finish you used on the beautiful salad bowl set you made for our anniversary?

SYLVIA: Well, Ben—that's a secret formula that's been in the family for generations. But, for some of that pecan fudge you and Alice make, I guess I could let you in on it. You'll have to swear not to reveal it to anyone, though.

BEN: Cross my heart and OK on the fudge.

SYLVIA: Get a pencil and paper. Here it is—the top-secret formula for non-toxic wood finish:

Step one: Get a tin can.

Step two: Pour in some walnut oil.

Step three: Send me the fudge.

Walnut oil is one answer to a difficult problem faced by toymakers: Many finishes are not safe for use on wooden toys.

The primary consideration in choosing a finish for a wooden toy is that it be safe for the youngster who might suck or chew on the toy. In order to be considered safe, the dried film must not contain toxic ingredients (especially heavy metals). The presence of lead in a toy finish is a main concern of the U.S. Consumer Product Safety Commission (an independent regulatory agency charged with reducing unreasonable risks of injury associated with consumer products). To prevent lead poisoning, they severely limit the amount of lead in toy paints and finishes to less than .06 percent.

The American National Standards Institute recognizes the danger of certain other metal ingredients used in paints. Among these are Antimony, Arsenic, Barium, Cadmium, Chromium, Mercury and Selenium. The Toy Manufacturers of America (the industry trade association) has established voluntary guidelines to limit the amount of metals in the toy paints they use.

There are several commercial wood-finish products which are considered child-safe for use on wooden toys.

Clear nitrocellulose lacquer consists of resins dissolved in a lacquer-thinner solvent. The solvent evaporates in minutes, leaving a protective topcoat which is water resistant. Lacquer is available in both spraying and brushing forms. Brushing lacquer contains additives to retard its drying time, allowing brush marks to disappear.

Latex varnish contains film-forming resins in a water base. Most brands dry overnight to a tough surface, which is more water-resistant than lacquer. Clean-up can be done with soap and water.

Shellac is a natural resin finish. It is available in a ready-to-apply mixture or in flakes which dissolve in denatured alcohol. The shelf life of both kinds is short, so shellac should be purchased in small quantities and used immediately. Shellac leaves a hard, glossy surface, which is moderately water-resistant.

Bowl finishes are oil/varnish products which have been approved by the U.S. Food and Drug Administration for use on surfaces that come into contact with food.

Natural oils, such as sunflower oil and walnut oil, provided excellent alternatives to commercial wood finishes. These pose no hazards to the child, the toymaker, or the environment. Sunflower oil and walnut oil penetrate the wood and harden to form a protective coating. Mineral oil and vegetable oil are sometimes used as toy finishes. They, too, penetrate the wood, but remain oily. All of these oils can be purchased at health food or grocery stores. They are easily applied with a brush, rag, or by dipping the toy into the oil. (Oil-soaked rags must be disposed of properly in order to avoid spontaneous combustion.) For an efficient way to oil large quantities of toys, see the automatic oiler in the section on commercial toymaking.

The fact that a finish is considered child-safe can be misleading. Just because a finish leaves a nontoxic surface coating on wood does not mean that the product is completely hazardless.

——Most commercial products, in liquid form, contain substances which are harmful or fatal if swallowed and must be kept out of the reach of children.

——The vapors given off by ingredients such as benzene, toluene, xylene, and petroleum distillates are hazardous to breathe, and in some cases are carcinogenic as well.

——Chemical additives present in many finishes can cause medical problems ranging from minor skin irritation to liver and kidney damage. Ideally, any commercial finish should be used outdoors with a vapor mask, gloves and goggles.

——Many people have concerns about the effect of hydrocarbons (contained in most commercial finishes) on the environment.

SAFETY RULES FOR CHOOSING A WOOD FINISH

1. Examine labels: Read warning labels, manufacturer recommendations, and ingredient lists.

2. Discard old or unlabeled finishes: Old finishes may not meet current safety and labeling requirements pertaining to hazardous ingredients.

3. Write to the manufacturer: If you have questions about a product's safety, ask the manufacturer for a product safety sheet.

4. Use only safe products: If you are not sure that a product is safe to use on a child's toy—*Don't use it!*

Toy Safety

Toys should be a source of joy rather than the cause of injury. It is the responsibility of the toymaker to be aware of potential safety hazards and to design and construct toys which are safe for the children for whom they are intended.

Regulations

The U.S. Government issues safety standards which must be followed by toy manufacturers. These standards are published as the *Code of Federal Regulations*, and are available through the Consumer Products Safety Commission (see appendix).

In addition to these mandatory standards, most toy manufacturers adhere to the *Voluntary Standards for Toy Safety*, which have been developed by the Toy Manufacturers of America.

Although intended for toy manufacturers, both the mandatory and the voluntary standards can be used to guide the craftsperson in making safe wood toys.

SMALL PARTS

As every parent knows, children constantly put things in their mouths . . . and ears . . . and noses. This is an especially common practice of children under three years of age. In order to minimize choking, aspiration, and ingestion hazards, the toymaker must avoid using small parts in toys for this age group. This rule applies to parts which could be broken off easily during play, as well as to parts which are intended to be detachable.

But how small is small? The Consumer Products Safety Commission uses a small-parts cylinder to test the size of toy parts. If a part fits entirely into this cylinder, it fails the test. It would not be considered safe for children under the age of three. If, on the other hand, it does not fit entirely into the cylinder, it passes the test (Illus. 32–33)

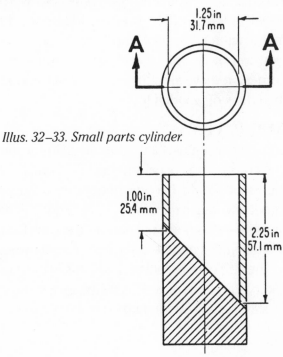

Illus. 32–33. Small parts cylinder.

21

CORDS AND STRINGS

Toys with long strings or cords can present strangulation hazards for babies and very young children. The danger is that the cord will become wrapped around a child's neck. Although these hazards are not addressed by the mandatory standards of the Consumer Products Safety Commission, they are covered by voluntary standards. These require that "flexible strings or cords greater than 12 inches long on pull toys intended for children less than three years of age not be provided with beads or other attachments that could tangle and form a loop."

The CPSC is also concerned about strings and cords attached to toys intended for cribs and playpens. The Voluntary Standards limits the length of these strings to 12 inches. It also limits the perimeter of any loop attached to these toys to 14 inches.

SHARP POINTS

The maker of wooden toys has less to worry about in terms of sharp edges than does the manufacturer of metal and hard plastic toys. However, it is still a good idea to round the corners, remove all splinters, and sand smooth the edges of wooden toys.

BABY RATTLES

The toymaker must take extra care in the design and construction of baby rattles. Toys which are too small could become lodged in a baby's throat and cause choking or suffocation. Small pieces used as noisemakers could escape from broken rattles and be aspirated or swallowed.

The size of baby rattles is addressed by mandatory standards as well as voluntary toy industry standards. The voluntary standards are even

more stringent than the government regulations and require that a rattle be large enough to prevent choking. A rattle complies with this standard only if the ends cannot penetrate the full depth of the opening in a test fixture 1.680″ in diameter, and 1.181″ deep. To be on the safe side, the ends of a rattle should be at least $1^{11}/_{16}$ inches in diameter. Illus. 34 shows a rattle with spherical ends of an appropriate size. The rattle should be built to withstand the rigorous play of an infant. Any small components used as noisemakers (mung beans work well) must be securely locked inside.

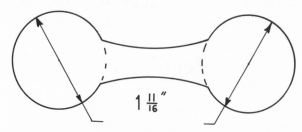

Illus. 34. Rattle.

PARENTAL RESPONSIBILITY

The toymaker alone cannot prevent toy-related accidents. Parents must share in the responsibility for toy safety. They can help by

—— Keeping toys intended for older children out of the hands of infants.

—— Teaching a child to use toys safely and preventing misuse of toys.

—— Repairing or discarding broken toys.

Building Durable Toys

Imagine the disappointment a child must feel when his new wooden toy disintegrates after a few minutes of vigorous play. Many people think that since wood is a durable material, a toy made of wood will naturally be durable—even unbreakable. But, of course, the strength of a toy depends as much upon the thought and care invested in its design and construction, as on the material used to make it. It is all too possible to make a fragile wood toy. A durable toy requires careful planning from the very start.

SELECTING THE WOOD

Some varieties of wood are more suitable for a particular toy piece. Consider the toaster toy design in this book. Although pine works well for the body of the toaster, it is best to use a stronger wood for the levers, as these pieces receive stress and are the most vulnerable. Maple, birch, or beech would be appropriate, as these woods resist splitting and are hard and durable. Selecting a wood which will hold up to the amount of stress a toy part receives results in a much more durable toy.

LAYING OUT THE PATTERN

Before marking a toy piece on a board, always think about the direction of the grain. Remember that the strongest part of wood is the grain fibre. In most cases, the longest dimension of a toy part should be laid out along the grain. This is especially important for long, narrow pieces, as these are liable to snap easily if cut with the grain going from side to side (Illus. 35).

 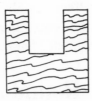

Right   Wrong

Illus. 35. Direction of wood grain.

Carefully examine the board for defects. Avoid cracks, as they are sure to weaken the structure of a toy. Although it is not always practical to avoid all knots (especially when working with pine) you should avoid loose knots and those which would take away from the structural integrity of the toy. Try to place any knots towards the center of a toy piece rather than on an edge.

ASSEMBLING THE PIECES

The next step in making a durable wood toy is to make sure that all of its pieces are securely fastened together.

Glue and clamps: Yellow carpenter's glue is preferable to ordinary white glue. The yellow glue is made specifically for joining wood. For maximum strength, glued surfaces should be placed under pressure while drying. A variety of clamps are available, which make it possible to clamp together almost any surfaces (Illus. 36–39).

 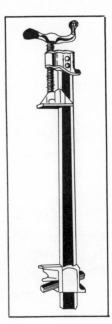

Illus. 36–38. Three examples of clamps.

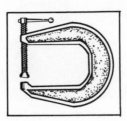

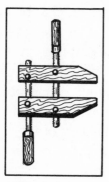

Illus. 39. Another kind of clamp.

Dowel pegs are also useful in toy assembly. These pegs can be bought precut and grooved or you can cut your own pegs from dowelling. The groove allows glue to be distributed along the length of the dowel rather than to be trapped at the bottom of the hole (Illus. 42).

Illus. 41. A heavy weight can provide adequate pressure for a strong glue joint.

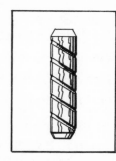

Illus. 42. Grooved dowel peg.

Woodscrews and nails: Although the use of woodscrews and nails is generally discouraged in the construction of wooden toys, they can be used when there is no danger that points will be exposed. They should be used in conjunction with glue, however, and not as a substitute. Used in this way, they squeeze the wood together for a proper glue joint and provide additional strength after the glue has dried.

Rounding Edges

Rounding the edges of a toy can improve the way it looks as well as the way it feels. Given enough time and elbow grease, rounding can

Illus. 40. The drill press can be used as a vise. Be sure to place a scrap of wood between the chuck and the toy to avoid marring.

be done with a carving tool, a rasp or even with coarse sandpaper. If you are interested in speed and accuracy, however, the router along with a corner-round router bit is the tool for you.

Corner-round router bits are available in radii from ³⁄₁₆ inch to ¾ inch and are made of either steel or carbide. Although carbide bits are more expensive, they last many times longer than ordinary steel bits and are more economical in the long run. A bit with a ⅜-inch radius is a good general-purpose bit for the toymaker to own. Choose a bit with a ball-bearing pilot rather than one with a fixed end. The pilot glides along the edge of the wood to control the depth of cut. A bearing allows for smoother operation, prevents marring and eliminates burning.

To round the edges of large flat pieces (such as game boards) the router is held by hand and is manipulated over the wood. To round the edges of smaller pieces, it is helpful to use a bench-mounted router. With the router attached to the bottom of a work table so that the bit protrudes through the table top, the wood can be manipulated against the router bit (Illus. 43–46).

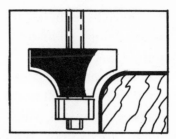

Illus. 44. A corner-round bit rounds the edge of wood.

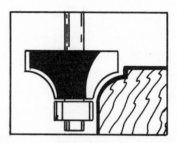

Illus. 45. Increasing the depth of cut will produce a single bead in addition to a rounded edge.

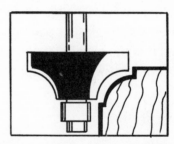

Illus. 46. By replacing the standard ball bearing with one of smaller diameter, a decorative double bead can be produced.

Sanding

Toymakers sometimes underestimate the importance of sanding the toys they make. The process of sanding a toy should be undertaken with as much care as any other toymaking operation.

Selecting the proper sandpaper: Sanding should begin with a coarse-grit abrasive and proceed through medium, fine, and very fine

Illus. 43. The end of a dowel can be rounded easily with a corner-round bit in a table-mounted router.

grit abrasives. Don't be tempted to skip grit steps—in the end it only will increase the time it takes to sand the toy.

Garnet is an orange abrasive paper, which is often preferred for sanding soft woods. Aluminum oxide is a brown abrasive, which works as well for sanding harder woods. Both kinds of abrasive paper come in grits from coarse to very fine.

Sandpaper also differs in the kind and weight of material that is used as a backing for the abrasive particles. A lightweight paper backing (designated with an "A") is used for lightweight hand-sanding. It tears easily, though, if used to sand irregular curves or when used on sanding machines. A heavier weight (C or D) paper or a cloth backing (X) is more appropriate for these more demanding applications. You can strengthen lightweight paper backings by covering them with plastic packaging tape. This ensures that the backing material lasts as long as the abrasive which it supports (Illus. 47).

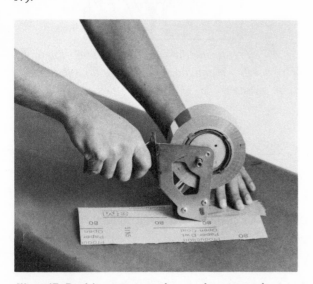

Illus. 47. Packing tape can be used to strengthen sandpaper backing.

Sanding small pieces: Electric finish-sanders are designed to be held by hand and manipulated over the surface of wood. Many toy pieces, however, are not large enough to sand in this manner. For these smaller pieces, it is more practical to turn the sander upside-down and to manipulate the wood over the vibrating abrasive. Use clamps or make a special fixture to temporarily attach the sander to the workbench (Illus. 48). A sander used in this manner needs to be cleaned out often, since sawdust will fall into the motor. Regularly blowing out the sawdust with compressed air prevents damage to the sander.

Illus. 48. An upside-down finish sander works well for sanding small toy parts.

Sanding inside curves: Sanding inside curves can be a frustrating task. The basic sanding machines are designed to sand outside surfaces and are useless for sanding the inside of holes and slots. But there is an alternative to hand-sanding these areas. Sanding drums come in an assortment of diameters and are ideal for sanding inside curves. The shaft of the sanding drum is mounted in the drill-press chuck. The abrasive sleeve can be changed quickly and easily.

If you do not own a set of sanding drums, you can make a quick, makeshift substitute by cutting a slit in a dowel and slipping in a short strip of cloth-backed abrasive (Illus. 49).

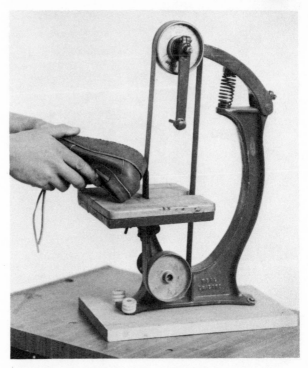

Illus. 50. An old shoe with a gum sole can be used to clean sanding belts.

Illus. 49. A homemade flap sander can be used to sand inside curves.

Cleaning sanding belts: The life of belts and discs can be extended by cleaning them with a special belt cleaner, which is a new product that looks much like a large gummy eraser. A similar material is used to make some shoe soles; so if you use up your belt cleaner, search your closet. You may find an old pair of sanding-belt cleaners you never dreamed you had (Illus. 50).

Burning and Branding

Whether you are putting spots on a toy giraffe, adding a handlebar moustache to a flying ace's face, or putting your signature on the bottom of a toy masterpiece, decorative burning may be preferable to painting. Several different tools and techniques can be used to burn details into wooden toys.

Woodburner: The woodburner is a versatile tool, which can be used to "draw" on wood. It usually comes with assorted tips, which can be screwed onto the standard point to create a variety of designs (Illus. 51).

Branding iron: There are two basic kinds of branding irons: Those with a self-contained

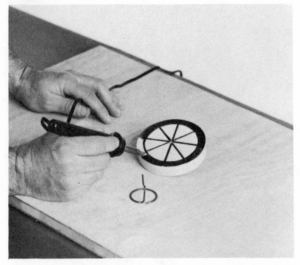

Illus. 51. The woodburner is ideal for adding detail to wood toys.

electric heating element and those requiring a secondary heat source. Branding heads can be custom-made with your name, message, or design cast in bronze or engraved in brass. Once the branding iron is heated, an unlimited number of identical brandings can be made (Illus. 52).

Illus. 52. This custom branding head was made for burning details into the camera toy.

Leathercraft stamps: Although intended for use in tooling leather, leathercraft stamps can be heated with a propane torch and used to brand decorative designs into wood. These tools come in hundreds of designs and cost only a few dollars each. Hold the tools with vise-grip pliers or make wooden handles to protect your hand from the hot metal (Illus. 53).

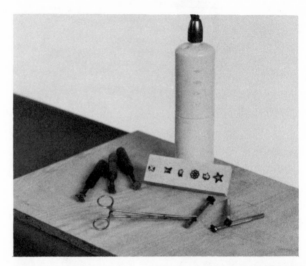

Illus. 53. Leathercraft stamps can also be used to burn designs into wood.

Propane torch: A propane torch can be used to burn wood. Shapes can be cut from sheet metal and placed on the toy to protect selected parts of the wood from the torch. By moving the torch quickly over the toy, exposed areas will be darkened (Illus. 54).

Hot metal: Experiment by heating bolts, screwdriver tips, copper tubing, and other metal objects to see what decorative designs can be made (Illus. 55).

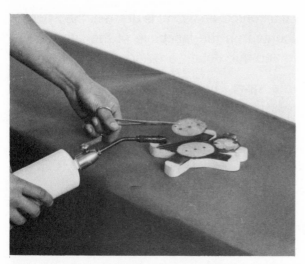

Illus. 54. The flame from a propane torch can be used to darken unprotected wood.

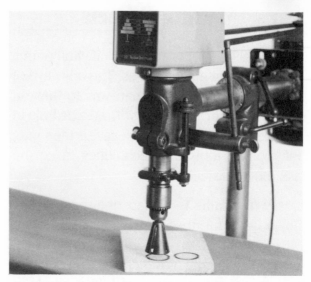

Illus. 56. This metal cone is made to drive a length of wood for shaping into a dowel. It is used here to burn ring patterns into wood.

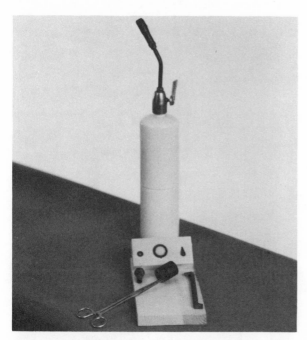

Illus. 55. An air-line plug, copper-pipe fitting and offset screwdriver were used to burn these designs.

Friction burning: Patterns can be burned into wood by using friction as a heat source. If you clamp a metal screw or nail into the drill-press chuck and bring the rotating head into contact with wood, enough heat will be produced to leave a burned impression (Illus. 56). A vari-

ation of this technique can be used to burn rings around a turned-wood piece. With the wood revolving on the lathe or in the drill press, a length of wire is wrapped around its circumference and pulled tight. A puff of smoke indicates that the burn has been accomplished. To avoid injury to hands, attach the wire ends to wooden handles (Illus. 57).

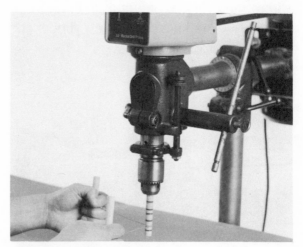

Illus. 57. A length of wire can be used to burn rings into wood handles.

Making Wheels

The wheel has not changed significantly since its invention in ancient times. The objective of the Mesopotamian craftsman was to make a smooth and circular wheel with an axle-hole in its exact center. Today the objective is the same, but modern tools and techniques make the task much easier.

Lathe: The lathe is perhaps the most ideally suited tool for the production of wooden wheels. With it, it is possible to turn a wheel from any wood of any dimension and contour. It is also ideal for accurately drilling a hole in the wheel's center and for sanding and polishing it to a mirror-like finish.

The stock is mounted on the lathe and rough-turned to the desired wheel diameter. The cylinder is then shaped into a number of individual wheels. The string of wheels can then be sanded with finer and finer grits of abrasive paper, rubbed with steel wool, and polished with a rag. A center hole is drilled to maximum depth into the impression left by the dead center of the lathe. The wheels are then cut from the cylinder, one at a time, and the center hole is redrilled into the cylinder as necessary (Illus. 58).

Illus. 58. Making wheels on a lathe.

If a contoured wheel is desired, the wheel is mounted on the faceplate of the lathe where tire and hub details are added.

Hole saw: The hole saw mounted in a drill press is a quick and accurate way of rough cutting wheels. A drill bit in the center of the saw automatically produces a perfectly centered axle hole. To avoid burning the wood, you should operate the drill press at a low speed. The saw is partially lowered until the drill bit penetrates the wood and the saw cuts about half of the way through. The stock is then turned over and the wheel is cut and extracted (Illus. 59).

Illus. 59. Using a hole saw to cut wheels.

The drill press can then be used to sand the wheel. A Phillips screwdriver bit is clamped into the chuck and press fit into the hole in the wheel. Abrasive paper can be held against the rotating wheel to speed sanding (Illus. 60).

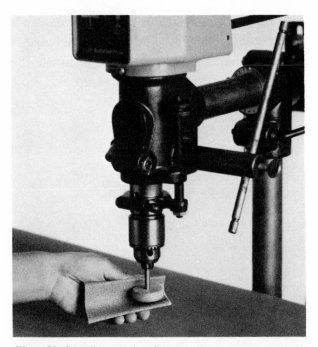

Illus. 60. Sanding a wheel.

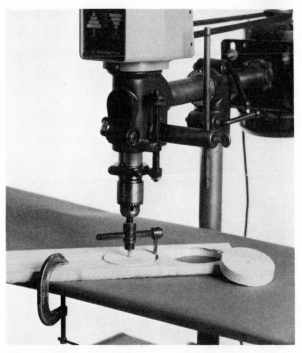

Illus. 61. Making a wheel with an adjustable circle cutter.

Adjustable circle cutter: The advantage of the adjustable circle cutter is that it can be set to cut wheels of various sizes. Once the blade has been set for the desired diameter, the tool is clamped into the drill press and used in the same way as the hole saw.

The circle cutter can be a dangerous tool and should be treated with respect. It should be used with the drill press operating at slow speed and the stock securely clamped to the drill-press table. A common accident occurs when the toymaker attempts to hold the stock by hand: The cutter head can bind and spin the wood into fingers and wrists (Illus. 61).

Bandsaw: The bandsaw is especially useful for cutting large diameter wheels. One method is to scribe a circle on the wood and use the bandsaw to cut it out free hand (Illus. 62). A faster, more accurate method is to use a jig clamped onto the bandsaw table. The jig is a pivot point at a desired distance from, and at a

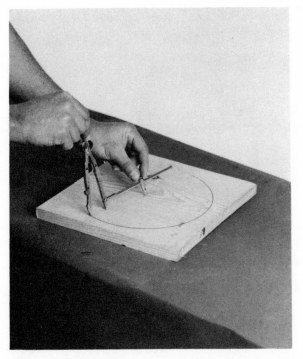

Illus. 62. Using a compass to mark a guideline.

right angle to, the blade. It can be as simple as a nail sticking up through a piece of plywood (Illus. 63). The piece of stock is pushed down over the nail and revolved while the blade cuts a perfect circle (Illus. 64).

Dowel wheels: A simple way to make wheels is to cut sections from a dowel or closet pole. A center square can then be used to locate the precise center for placement of an axle hole (Illus. 65).

Illus. 63. Look closely at this photo to see the pivot point in this simple circle jig.

Illus. 65. Cutting wheels from a length of dowel.

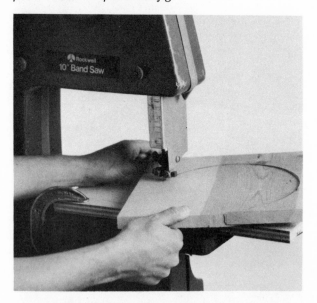

Illus. 64. By rotating a piece of wood on this pivot point, a perfect wheel can be made.

Commercial wheels: The recent popularity of toymaking has increased the availability of commercially turned wheels (as well as other toy parts). Wheels are now available in an assortment of colors, woods, dimensions and styles, including the latest spoked wheels.

Train (also shown on cover) comes equipped with both cowcatcher and cow. It also possesses an engineer and a coal man who moves. The train is in three sections: engine, coal car and caboose. Directions start on page 96.

A key to the toy parts on left can be found on page 127.

A

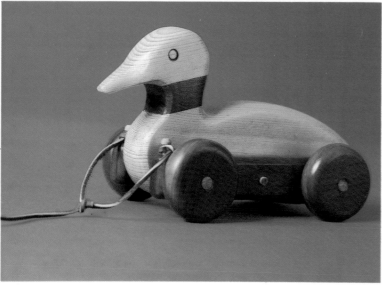

Trojan Horse pull toy (above) has two surprise passengers inside. Directions start on page 34.

Duck pull toy on left follows along with a bobbing motion. Instructions for it start on page 52.

B

The Don Quixote above is made so that he tilts back and forth (though not necessarily at windmills). Directions start on page 45.

Directions for the easy-to-make cradle on the right start on page 49.

The pop-up toaster on the left really does pop up toast although it is not edible. Directions which start on page 67 also include instructions for making the "toast."

Watch out for the birdie on the left! It keeps trying to get into the picture. Directions which start on page 63, also include a picture of the upside-down birdie.

D

Directions for the dump truck on the right start on page 76.
A lever trips the hinged bed and a peg in the front axle keeps the "driver" bouncing.

The iron set below is a quick-and-easy project. Directions start on page 70.

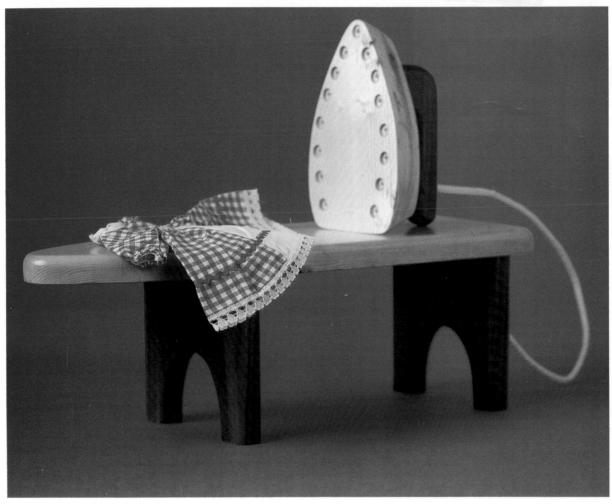

E

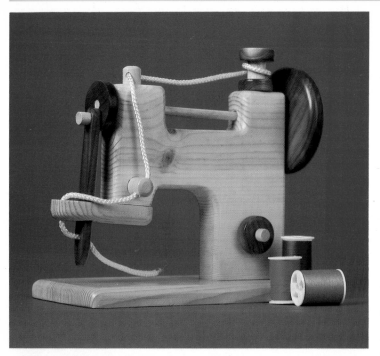

Instructions for the sewing machine on the upper left start on page 37. The sewing-machine needle moves up and down.

The robot above is far easier to make than it appears. Instructions start on page 91. This robot has little to say, although his mouth opens, but he can easily be made to move with just a push.

The rocking pig on the left is not just for riding. He's a huge piggy bank or a great place for a child to hide treasures. Instructions start on page 58.

As the big horn pull toy on the right is pulled along, the two rams rear and strike their horns together. Instructions start on page 80.

The telephone on the left should not only keep a child "busy," but provide no "wrong numbers." Instructions start on page 55.

This buzz saw makes a buzzing noise as the wheel moves. Instructions start on page 41.

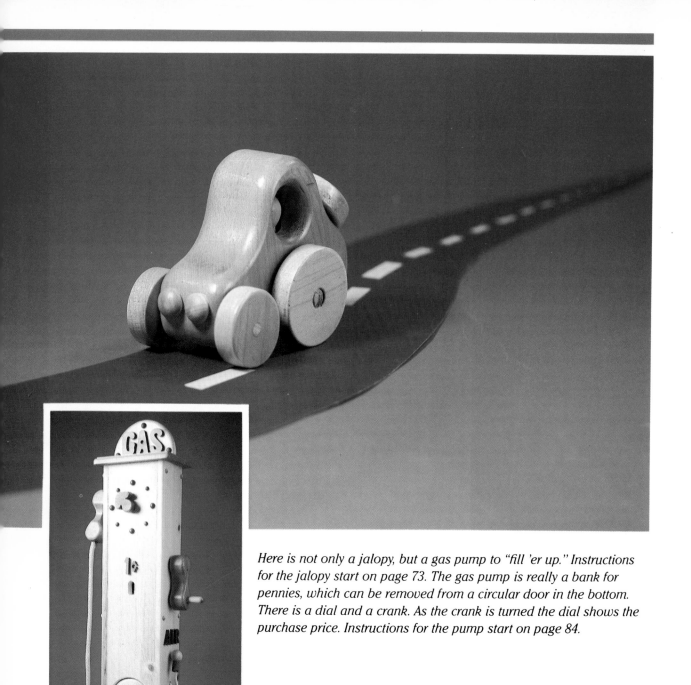

Here is not only a jalopy, but a gas pump to "fill 'er up." Instructions for the jalopy start on page 73. The gas pump is really a bank for pennies, which can be removed from a circular door in the bottom. There is a dial and a crank. As the crank is turned the dial shows the purchase price. Instructions for the pump start on page 84.

H

2
TOYS

Our Toy Plans

Every toy designer develops an individual style based on a personal toymaking philosophy. The toys in this section were designed with the following thoughts in mind:

——A toy should invite children to participate and should not do the playing for them.

——A good toy encourages joyful, cooperative play rather than violent, aggressive play.

——A toy with a minimum amount of detail provides more stimulation for a child's imagination than does a highly detailed toy.

——It is difficult to improve upon the natural beauty of wood. In most cases, a clear finish is more desirable than one that obscures the wood. When color is needed, a nontoxic wood stain is used.

With these plans, we have attempted to provide all the necessary information for duplicating the toys as we made them. There is no reason, however, that you need to stick to the plans. Feel free to add your own ideas. Use different kinds of wood. Change the shape, or change the dimensions. Better yet, use the toys to spark new toy ideas of your own.

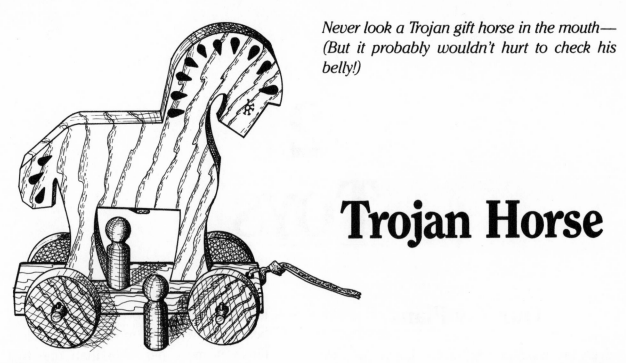

Never look a Trojan gift horse in the mouth— (But it probably wouldn't hurt to check his belly!)

Trojan Horse

Illus. 66.

TROJAN HORSE

Just as in the legend, this stately wood horse contains a hidden surprise. Just twist the latch to release a pair of stowaways.

HORSE

Begin by marking pattern (A) on ¾ hardwood and cutting out the horse profile. Bore the 1″ dia. flat-bottomed holes in the horse as indicated by the arrows on the pattern.

Drill a ⁵⁄₃₂″ dia. latch hole as indicated. Now cut out the platform (H) from ¼ hardwood. Drill ⅜″-dia. and ¾″ deep axle holes 1¼″ from each end of the base. Drill ¼″-dia. pull-string hole through the front of the base.

Cut the latch (B) from a hardwood scrap and drill a ³⁄₁₆″ hole in its center. Sand the horse, base and latch. Next, attach the latch to the horse, using a glued pivot peg. Now, glue the

horse to the base and when dry, reinforce this joint with glue pins. Using a woodburner, burn details on the horse.

WHEELS

To make the wheels, use an adjustable circle cutter and cut four 2¼″-dia. circles from ¼ hardwood. Enlarge the center hole in each wheel to ⁷⁄₁₆″ dia. and sand.

From ⅜″-dia. dowelling, cut the four axle pieces (F) to length and drill a ³⁄₁₆″-dia. hole near the end of each. From ³⁄₁₆″-dia. dowelling, cut four axle pegs (G) and glue them into these axle holes.

Insert pegged axles through wheels and glue into holes in the base, leaving enough clearance so that the wheels spin freely. Finally, attach the pull cord (see Toy Safety Considerations) and insert the Greeks (D).

34

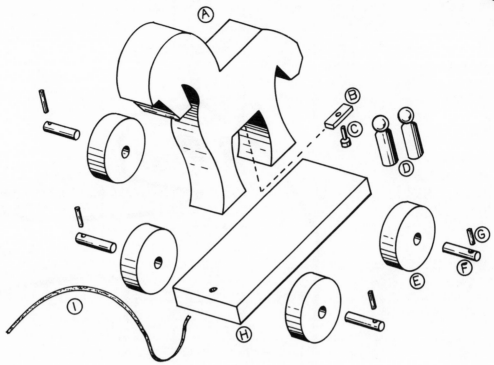

Illus. 67. Assembly of parts for Trojan Horse.

MATERIALS LIST

Ref.	No. of Pieces	Thickness in inches	Width in inches	Length in inches	Material
A	1	1¾	8½	8	maple
B	1	¼	⅜	1⅜	black walnut
C			⁵⁄₃₂ dia.	¹³⁄₁₆	peg
D	2		¾ dia.	2⁵⁄₁₆	people turning*
E	4	¹³⁄₁₆	2¼ dia.		maple
F	4		⅜ dia.	1¾	dowel
G	4		³⁄₁₆ dia.	⅝	dowel
H	1	¹³⁄₁₆	3	9	black walnut
I	1				cord

*"People turning" refers to a part made on the lathe which also can be purchased ready-made.

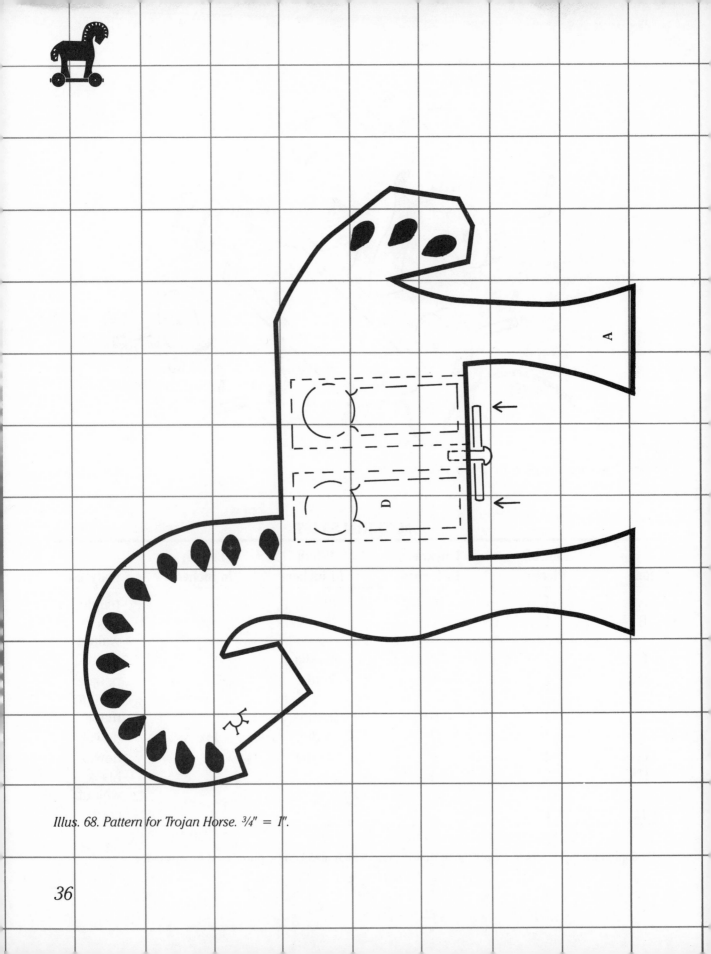

Illus. 68. Pattern for Trojan Horse. ³/₄″ = 1″.

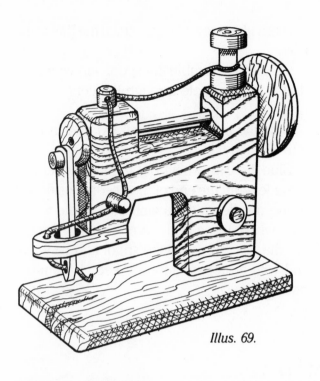

Illus. 69.

Keep the kids in stitches
Sewing imaginary rips in britches.

Sewing Machine

SEWING MACHINE

A wheel cam changes the circular motion to an up-and-down movement of the needle.

CUT THE PIECES

From 2 × pine, cut the body (B). Cut the needle guide (E) and the base (D) from 1 × pine. There are five wheels to be cut using an adjustable circle cutter. The first (A) is 4½″ in diameter and is cut from ¼ hardwood. Three 1½″-dia. wheels (C) are cut from ½″-thick hardwood. The last wheel (H) is cut from ⁷⁄₁₆″-thick hardwood, with the circle cutter set to a 2″-dia. (Commercial wheels are also available in these sizes.)

Cut the needle (G) from ⅜″-thick hardwood. Cut a length of ⅜″-dia. dowel for axle (J). For spool center (L) cut a 1¼″ length of ¾″-dia. dowel. Then cut a length of ⅜″ dowel for the spool post (K).

Cut the two thread guides (I) from a ¾″-dia. dowel.

ROUND THE EDGES

Round one surface of the needle guide and one surface of the base. Round both surfaces of the wheel (A). Round all but the two glue edges of the sewing-machine body. Round one end of each thread guide. Then sand all pieces.

DRILL THE HOLES

The holes in the body should be drilled as follows:

Two shallow ¾″-dia. holes for the thread guides.

One ⅜″-dia. hole for the spool post.

For axle (J) drill ⁷⁄₁₆″-dia. holes in both ends of the body as indicated by arrows on the pattern.

One ¼″-dia. hole for the dial.

Drill ¼″-dia. holes in the thread guides.

One ¼″-dia. hole in the cam wheel (H), ⅝ of an inch from the center point.

One ¼″-dia. hole in the needle guide (E) for the thread. Drill a 1″-dia. hole in the needle guide and round the edges of this hole on both sides.

Drill a 5/16"-dia. hole in the top of the needle. To make the eye of the needle, drill two closely spaced 1/4"-dia. holes and remove the remaining stock with a small chisel or a coping saw.

Enlarge the center holes in wheels (A) and (H) to 3/8"-dia. Enlarge the center hole in one wheel (C) to 5/16"-dia. Drill shallow 3/4"-dia. holes in two of the wheels (C).

ASSEMBLE

Glue the needle guide to the body.

Glue the base to the body. Use glue pegs or screws to strengthen this joint.

Attach and glue the thread guides and spool post to the body.

Use a glued pivot peg to attach the dial to the body.

Glue and assemble the spool and when dry, drill a 7/16"-dia. hole through the center of the unit.

Glue the axle (J) to wheel (A) and insert it into the body.

Glue the cam wheel (H) to the other end of the axle. With the end of the needle positioned in the needle guide, attach the needle to the cam wheel using a glued pivot peg. Attach a 3/16"-dia. nylon cord to the spool and heat one end with a propane torch to keep it from unraveling.

MATERIALS LIST

Ref.	No. of Pieces	Thickness in inches	Width in inches	Length in inches	Material
A	1	13/16	4 1/2 dia.		black walnut
B	1	1 1/2	7 1/2	8 3/8	pine
C	3	1/2	1 1/2 dia.		black walnut
D	1	3/4	5 1/2	11	pine
E	1	3/4	1 1/2	4 1/4	pine
F	2		1/4 dia.		pivot peg
G	1	3/8	3/4	6	black walnut
H	1	7/16	2 dia.		black walnut
I	2		3/4 dia.	1 1/4	dowel
J	1		3/8 dia.	9 7/8	dowel
K	1		3/8 dia.	2	dowel
L	1		3/4 dia.	1 1/4	dowel
	1		3/16 dia.	18	cord

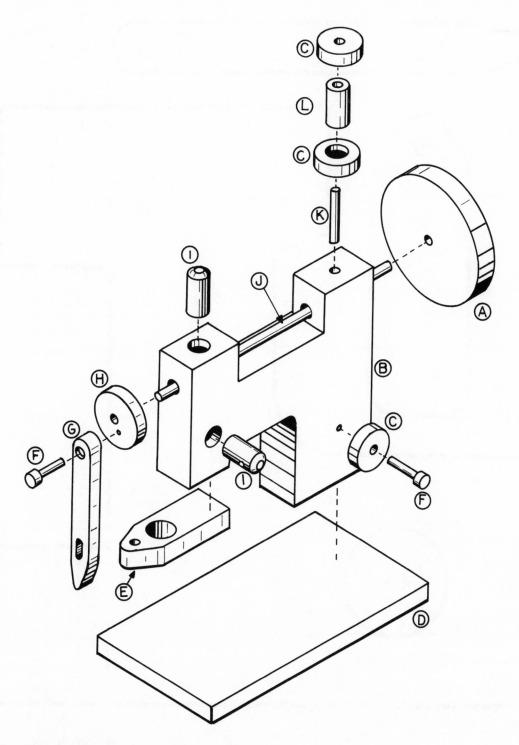

Illus. 70. Assembly of parts for sewing machine.

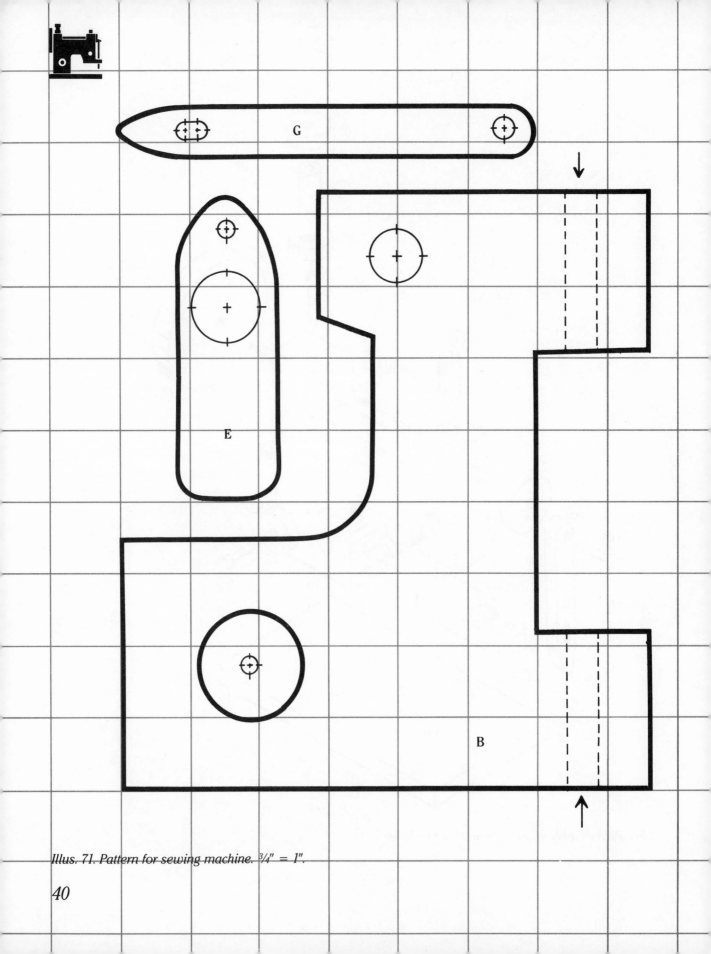

Illus. 71. Pattern for sewing machine. ³⁄₄″ = 1″.

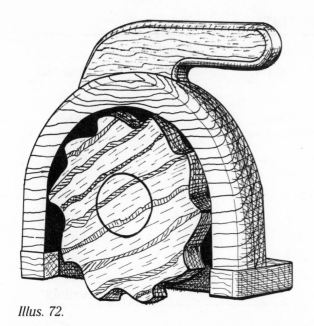

Illus. 72.

Pushed on a board
To cut fast and square,
Imaginary sawdust
Flies through the air.

Buzz Saw

BUZZ SAW

The simple sound mechanism used on this toy is a variation of the old playing card in the bicycle spokes. A wheel rides against any surface to turn the blade.

CONSTRUCTION

Except for the ¼ hardwood blade, the buzz saw is made from 1 × pine. Use the patterns to cut out these pieces. Use an adjustable circle cutter to cut the 4½″-dia. drive wheel.

Round around the outside edges of (I) and (C), but do not round the glue edges. Round around one side of (G) except for the bottom glue joint and, on the blade side, round around the handle only.

Drill shallow ³⁄₁₆″-dia. holes in (C) as shown on pattern.

Cut ¾″ lengths of dowel and glue into these holes. Sand all parts.

Drill a ¹³⁄₁₆″-dia. axle hole through (G) and (C). Drill a ¾″-dia. flat-bottomed hole into the inside center of (A) and (J). Drill ¼″-dia. holes in (H).

Cut a 3⅜″ length of ¾″-dia. dowel for axle (B). Using pattern (E), cut a piece of flexible plastic from a coffee can lid or butter tub.

ASSEMBLY

Glue together the sound-box pieces (F) and (C). Clamp and set aside to dry.

Cut a 2¹⁄₁₆-in. slit in the axle. Insert plastic piece (E) in the axle and secure with small nails or staple.

Glue and clamp together blade guard (I) and saw body(G).

Glue and position noise-box unit to body (J), making certain that the axle moves freely. Clamp and allow to dry. Glue and attach wheel, blade and base.

MATERIALS LIST

Ref.	No. of Pieces	Thickness in inches	Width in inches	Length in inches	Material
A	1	¾	4½ dia.		pine
B	1		¾ dia.	3⅜	dowel
C	1	¾	4½	4	pine
D	7		³⁄₁₆ dia.	¾	dowel
E	1		⅝	2¾	plastic
F	1	¾	4½	4	pine
G	1	¾	7¼	6½	pine
H	1	¾	3	7¼	pine
I	1	¾	7¼	5	pine
J	1	¾	5⅜ dia.		black walnut

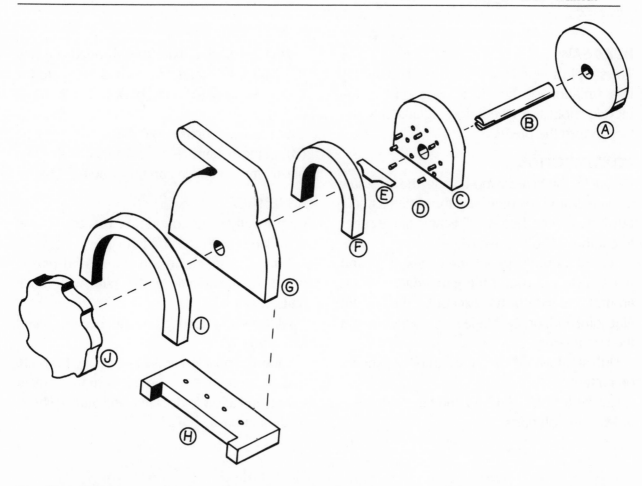

Illus. 73. Assembly of parts for buzz saw.

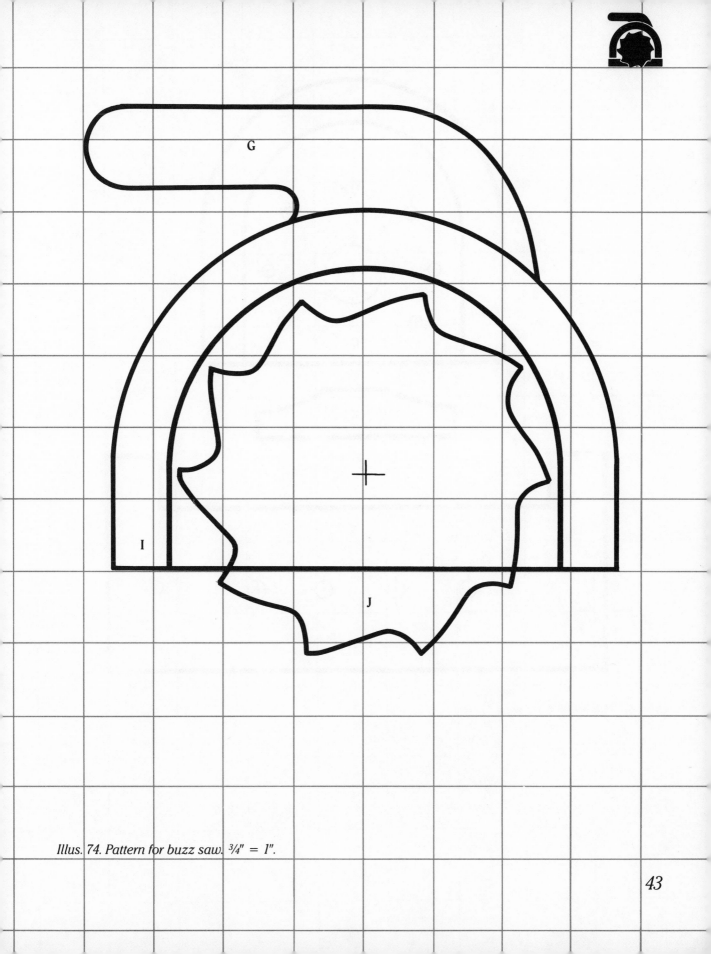

G

I

J

Illus. 74. Pattern for buzz saw. ¾" = 1".

43

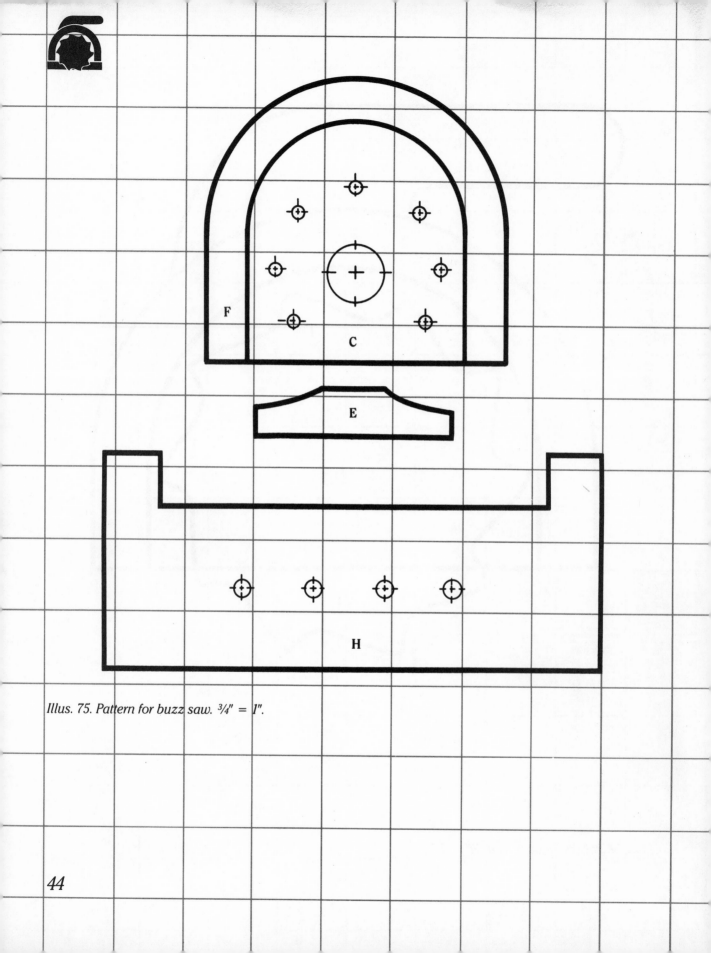

Illus. 75. Pattern for buzz saw. ¾" = 1".

Illus. 76.

Tilting at windmills
They're quite a sight—
Rickety old steed
And tall, scraggy knight.

Don Quixote

DON QUIXOTE

The front wheels of this toy are drilled off-center so that the horse rises and falls as it's pulled along. Don Quixote is attached to the horse's back with a loose-fitting pin. As he tilts back and forth, lance in hand, he appears to be spurring the horse into a charge.

RIDER

Begin by using pattern (D) to mark and cut the horseman's body from ¼ hardwood. Round and shape the shoulder area as shown in side-view pattern (D). Round back edges of Don Quixote.

HORSE

Use pattern (F) to mark the horse on ¼ hardwood, then cut.

Round all edges of the horse. Drill two ⁷⁄₁₆″-dia. axle holes and a ⁵⁄₁₆″ pivot hole in the horse.

HEAD

Using pattern (K) mark the head on ¼ hardwood, then cut. Drill a ¼″-dia. neck hole in the head as indicated on pattern (K).

HAT

To make Don Quixote's hat, drill a shallow ½″-dia. hole in a 1½″-dia. wheel and glue in a dowel button.

DRILL

Drill two ¼″-dia. holes in body for lance (C) and neck (N). Position and angle are shown on side-view pattern (D).

Drill a ¼″-dia. hole for pivot dowel (E). Drill ⁷⁄₃₂″-dia. holes for shield peg (B) and for pull-cord peg (P).

DOWELS

Cut sections of ¼″-dia. dowel to length for lance, neck, and pivot (E). Drill ¼″-dia. hole in a

⅜" wood ball and glue it to tip of lance. Cut two ¾"-dia. dowels to length for the rear-axle spacers and drill a ⁷⁄₁₆"-dia. hole through the center of each. Use short lengths of dowel to plug the centers of the two front wheels and then re-drill the axle hole slightly off-center to a depth of ½".

ASSEMBLY

Sand all pieces. Attach lance, shield, and head to Don Quixote. Position on horse and insert pivot dowel (E). Attach wheels.

Note: Spacers on the rear axle add stability. Align front wheels before gluing to axle. Attach cord. (See Toy Safety Considerations.)

MATERIALS LIST

Ref.	No. of Pieces	Thickness in inches	Width in inches	Length in inches	Material
A	1	⁹⁄₁₆	1¾ dia.	1¼	wheel
B	1		⁷⁄₃₂ dia.	1¼	peg
C	1		¼ dia.	6	dowel
D	1	¹³⁄₁₆	2⅜	5⅛	black walnut
E	1		¼ dia.	2⅜	dowel
F	1	¹³⁄₁₆	6¼	6½	maple
G	2		¾ dia.	1	dowel
H	1		⅜ dia.	4⁷⁄₁₆	dowel
I	1		⅜ dia.	1¹⁵⁄₁₆	dowel
J	1		⅜ dia.		wood ball
K	1	¹³⁄₁₆	1	1⅛	maple
L	1	½	1½ dia.		wheel
M	1		½ dia.		button
N	1		¼ dia.	1	dowel
O	4	¾	2¼ dia.		wheel
P	1		⁷⁄₃₂ dia.	1¼	peg
Q	1				cord

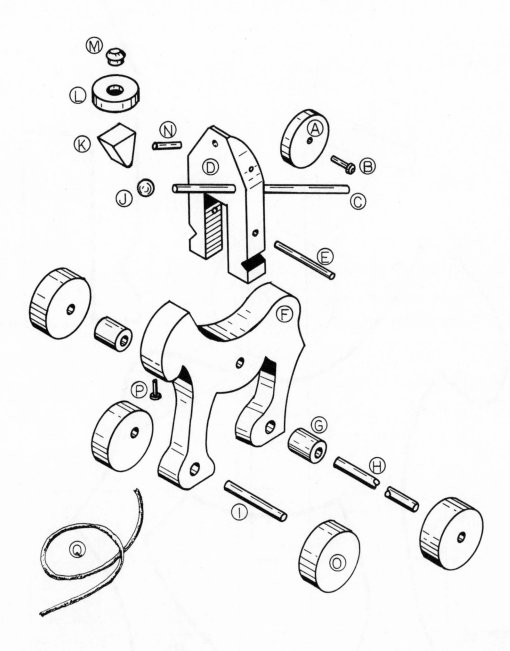

Illus. 77. Assembly of parts for Don Quixote.

Illus. 78. Pattern for Don Quixote. ¾" = 1".

48

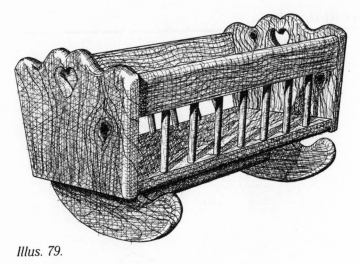

Illus. 79.

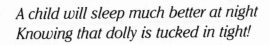

*A child will sleep much better at night
Knowing that dolly is tucked in tight!*

Cradle

CRADLE
The cradle is designed to be easily built from 1 × 12 pine and includes no complicated joints or angle cuts.

BODY
Using pattern (D), mark and cut the end pieces of the cradle. Drill the ⅜″ and ¾″ decorative heart-holes in these pieces as indicated on the pattern. Use a jigsaw or coping saw to remove the remaining stock. Round around all but the inside glue edges.

Cut two rails (A) and one cradle bottom (C). Using pattern (A), mark the position of ⅜″-dia. dowel holes on the rails (A) and the cradle bottom (C). Now drill holes in the rail to a depth of ¾″. Drill ½″-deep holes in the bottom of the cradle at an 80° angle so that the slant of the rails will match the slant of the ends.

Round the top edges of the rails (A) and the bottom edges of (C). Do not round the glue edges. Sand all parts.

ROCKERS
Using pattern (F), mark and cut out the two rockers and round all but the glue edge. Cut one rocker support (E) and round bottom edges. Sand these parts.

ASSEMBLY
Cut fourteen lengths of ⅜″-dia. dowels, glue and insert them into the rails. Put a small amount of glue in cradle bottom holes. Align the assembled rail units with these holes and gently tap into place.

Glue on cradle ends and clamp with bar clamps. Glue the rockers to the rocker support (E) and clamp. When the glue is dry, glue and attach the rockers to the cradle. Strengthen all joints with glue pins or countersunk wood screws.

49

MATERIALS LIST

Ref.	No. of Pieces	Thickness in inches	Width in inches	Length in inches	Material
A	2	¾	2	16½	pine
B	14		⅜ dia.	4	dowel
C	1	¾	8	16½	pine
D	2	¾	9⅞	7	pine
E	1	¾	2	10	pine
F	2	¾	3⅛	10¼	pine

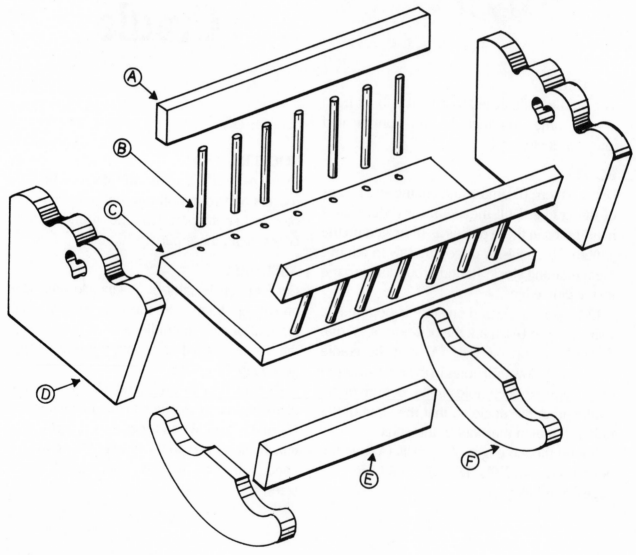

Illus. 80. Assembly of parts for cradle.

50

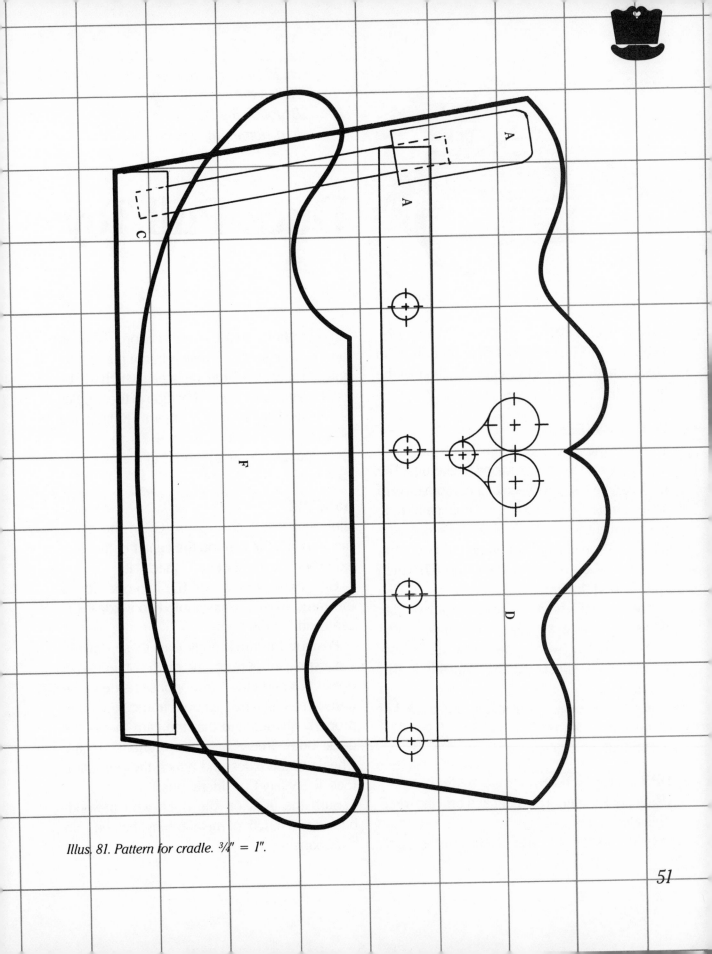

Illus. 81. Pattern for cradle. ³/₄″ = 1″.

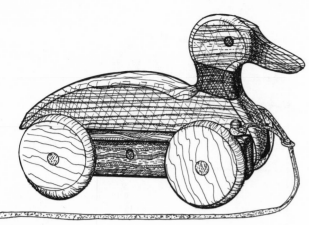

Illus. 82.

Build Duckie with care—
He'll return your devotion,
By following feet
In a swimming motion.

Duck Pull Toy

DUCK PULL TOY

The secret to this toy's bobbing motion is an offset length of dowel or cam attached to the front axle.

CUT THE PIECES

To build the duck, glue up the 2 pieces of 2 × pine and the ¼ hardwood neck-ring. (The neck can be a single piece or a combination of small strips of hardwood.) Using pattern E, mark and cut out the body. Now, mark the frame pieces (B) on ¼ hardwood and cut them out. Next, cut ⅜″-dia. dowels to length for (D) which will support the frame.

The cam (F) is cut to length from ⅞″-dia. doweling. Using an adjustable circle cutter, make 2¼″-dia. wheels from ¼ hardwood. (Commercial wheels are also available in this diameter.)

Round all edges and shape the duck bill using a knife or rasp.

Sand all the pieces.

DRILL THE HOLES

Using duck pattern (E), mark and drill the three indicated holes.

Using pattern (B), mark and drill the three indicated holes in the frame sections. Now, on the top front surface of each frame piece, drill holes to accept ⁵⁄₃₂″-dia. pivot peg which will be used to attach the cord. (Position of these holes is indicated by arrow on pattern.) Enlarge the holes in the center of the wheels to ⅜″ dia. Using pattern (F), mark and drill the off-center cam hole.

ASSEMBLY

Glue and insert cord pegs (G) in the frame pieces. Glue the cam on the center of the front axle (being careful not to "quack" it).

Glue the ¼″-dia. dowel (D) into one side of the frame. Insert the assembled front axle in the same side of the frame.

Position the duck body over these dowels. Put a small amount of glue on the other end of dowel (D) and attach the opposite side of the frame, making sure that both frame pieces are properly aligned and that the cam moves the duck body freely between them. Glue the wheels to the axles and attach the pull cord. (See Toy Safety Considerations.)

Burn the eyes on the duck with a wood-burner or a length of metal tubing, heated with a propane torch.

MATERIALS LIST

Ref.	No. of Pieces	Thickness in inches	Width in inches	Length in inches	Material
A	4	¹³⁄₁₆	2¼ dia.		maple
B	2	¹³⁄₁₆	1¼	7	cherry
C	2		⅜ dia.	4⅞	dowel
D	1		¼ dia.	3³⁄₁₆	dowel
E	1	1½	4⅞	9½	pine & cherry
F	1		⅞ dia.	¾	dowel
G	2		⁵⁄₃₂ dia.		peg
H	1				leather cord

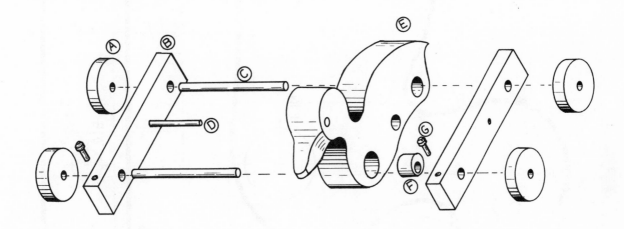

Illus. 83. Assembly of parts for duck pull toy.

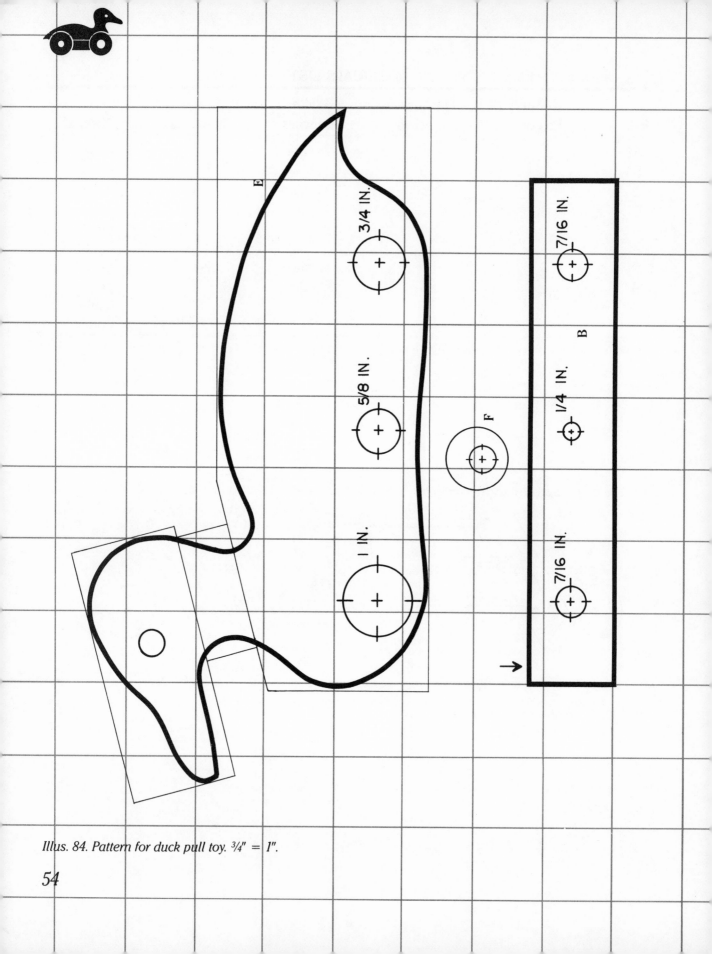

Illus. 84. Pattern for duck pull toy. ¾″ = 1″.

Illus. 85.

Whether used to conduct serious business conversations, or just to call up and say "hello," this wooden phone will provide a "hot line" to a child's imagination.

Telephone

TELEPHONE

Before making this toy, it's a good idea to search through the scrap bin to find a variety of woods. The more color and contrast, the better.

CONSTRUCTION

Use the patterns to mark the receiver (A) and the hooks (H) on ¼ hardwood. Cut out these pieces and round the top edge of the receiver. Next, use pattern (F) to mark the base on 2 × pine, and cut out this piece with the bandsaw table set at 23°.

Use an adjustable circle cutter to cut two 1¾"-dia. receiver pieces (B) from ¼ hardwood. Round one edge of each circle. Readjust the circle cutter to cut one 2½"-dia. circle from ⅜"-thick hardwood. Then using the pattern, mark and drill the ⅜"-dia. holes around the circumference of the dial. Sand all pieces. Now enlarge the hole in the center of this dial to ⁵⁄₁₆".

ASSEMBLY

To mount the dial, drill a ¼"-dia. hole perpendicular to the front of the base (F). Attach the dial with a glued pivot peg.

Glue the receiver hooks to the base and when the glue has set, drill ¼"-dia. holes and insert glue pegs (I). Glue the receiver pieces (B) to receiver (A), and when dry, drill holes and insert glue pegs (C).

To include a cord (optional), drill holes through the centers of two ½" screw-hole buttons, thread them onto a cord and knot the cord ends. (See Toy Safety Considerations.)

MATERIALS LIST

Ref.	No. of Pieces	Thickness in inches	Width in inches	Length in inches	Material
A	1	$^{13}/_{16}$	1¾	5⅞	black walnut
B	2	$^{13}/_{16}$	1½ dia.		maple
C	2		¼ dia.	1¼	dowel
D	1		¼		peg
E	1	⅜	2½ dia.		black walnut
F	1	1½	3⅞	5	pine
G	1		$^{3}/_{16}$ dia.	12	cord
H	2	$^{13}/_{16}$	1¾	1¾	black walnut
I	2		¼ dia.	1½	dowel
J	2		½ dia.		screw-hole buttons

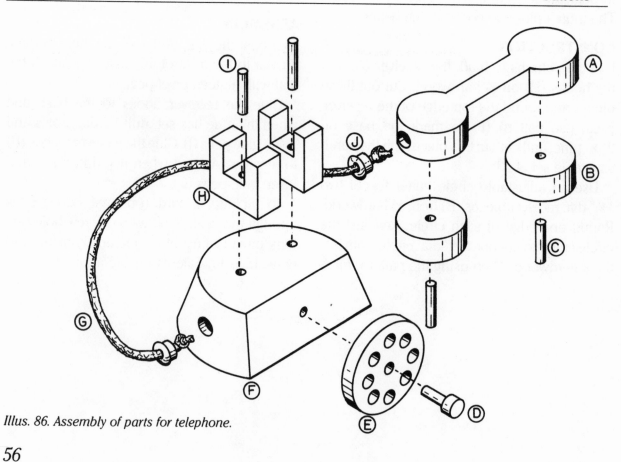

Illus. 86. Assembly of parts for telephone.

56

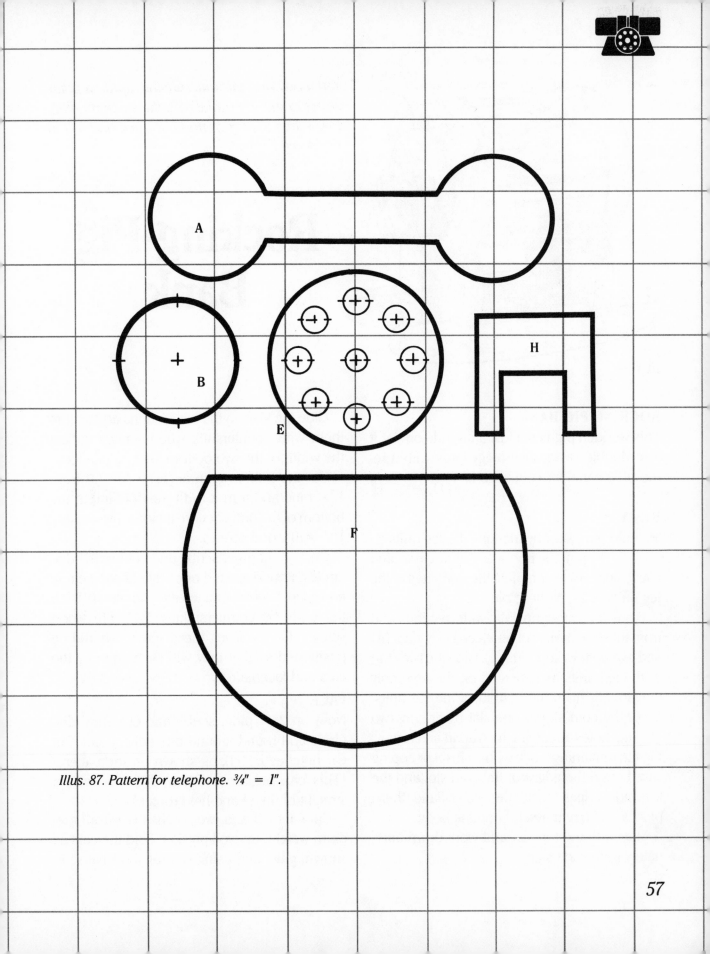

Illus. 87. Pattern for telephone. ¾" = 1".

Illus. 88.

You won't find this enterprising, uptown piggy going to market (unless it's the stock market). He prefers to stay at home to rock and roll in the dough!

Rocking-Pig Bank

ROCKING PIG BANK

This wooden pig is not just a fun ride-on toy. It also doubles as a huge piggy bank with a removable panel for coin access.

BODY

To build him, start by marking the leg units (I) on 2 × 10 pine; scribe a 9¼″-dia. circle and use the pattern to complete the lower half of the leg units. Cut out these pieces.

From 1 × pine, rip 1³⁄₁₆″-wide sections and from these sections cut nineteen body slats (A) and two bottom supports (L). Glue the two (L's) to the leg units as indicated on the assembly drawing, 8″ from the bottom of the leg units. Make the coin slot in one slat by drilling two ⁷⁄₁₆″-dia. holes about one inch apart and removing the remaining stock with a chisel or coping saw. Round the edges of the coin slot and the top side edges of all the slats. Sand these pieces and begin assembling the body.

Start with the top slat and work down alternately from each side.

Glue the slats to the leg sections and secure them with countersunk wood screws. Adjust the width of the two bottom slats as needed.

Cut the bottom coin access plate (J) from 1 × pine and trim it to fit the opening in the bottom of the body. Secure it by countersinking 1½″ #10 wood screws.

On 1 × 12 pine, scribe and cut two 11″-dia. circles. Round around one edge of each circle and sand. Glue and attach the end plates (D) to the body by countersinking 1½″ #10 wood screws. On the front, these screws should be positioned so that they will be hidden by the ears and faceplate.

FACE

Now, on 2 × pine, scribe and cut an 8″-dia. circle and round around one edge. Sand. Cut ear notches in (H), as shown on the pattern. (This can be done with a chisel or with a straight bit in a hand-held router.)

Cut ears (E) and eye patches (C) from medium-weight, undyed pigskin. Fold the ears as shown, glue, and using several short nails, attach the ears securely to the back of the faceplate.

Glue and attach the faceplate to the front-end plate by countersinking 2″ #10 wood screws. These screws should be positioned so that they will be hidden by the eye patches and snout.

Use pattern (G) to mark the snout on 2 × pine and cut it out with the bandsaw table set at 23°. Drill 1″-dia. holes, ¾ of an inch deep for nostrils. Drill a ³⁄₁₆″-dia. hole in the center of each of these holes. Sand the snout, glue and attach it to the face with 2″ #10 wood screws. Use thin sections of 1″ dowel to cover screws.

ROCKERS

Using pattern (K), mark and cut the rockers from 2 × pine. Sand, glue, and attach them to the body with 2″ #10 wood screws, using a countersinking drill bit.

FINISHING TOUCHES

Cut two 1½″ wide pigskin strips, approximately 36″ long.

Glue and attach as shown on the assembly drawing. Secure these leather strips with small pivot pegs. Glue on eye patches. Use a section of tubing that has been warmed over a propane torch to burn on the eyes.

MATERIALS LIST

Ref.	No. of Pieces	Thickness in inches	Width in inches	Length in inches	Material
A	19	¾	1³⁄₁₆	12	pine
B	2		1½	36	pigskin
C	2	(see pattern)			pigskin
D	2	¾	11 dia.		pine
E	2	(see pattern)			pigskin
F	9	#10		2	wood
	48	#10		1½	screws
G	1	1½	4½		pine
H	1	1½	8 dia.		pine
I	2	1½	9¼	15¾	pine
J	1	¾	5½	9	pine
K	2	1½	3	22	pine
L	2	¾	1³⁄₁₆	5	pine
M	7		½ dia.		screw-hole buttons
N	14		³⁄₁₆ dia.		pivot pegs

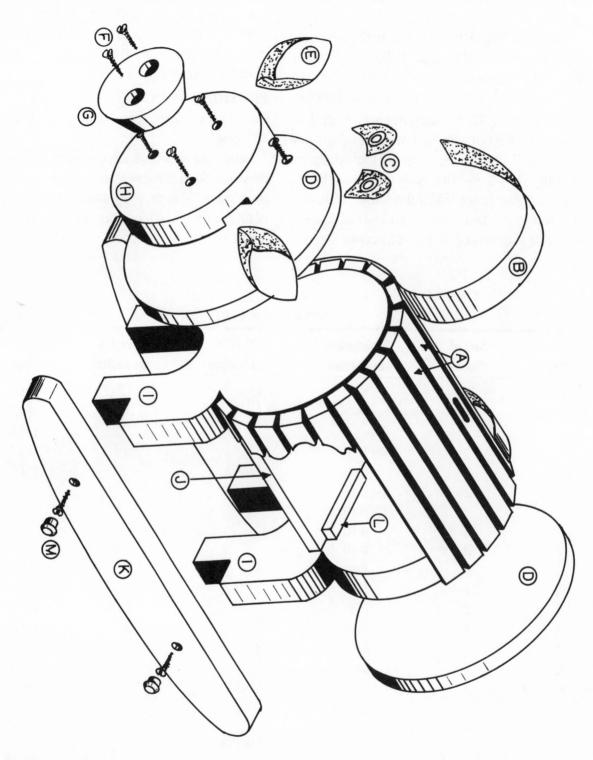

Illus. 89. Assembly of parts for rocking-pig bank.

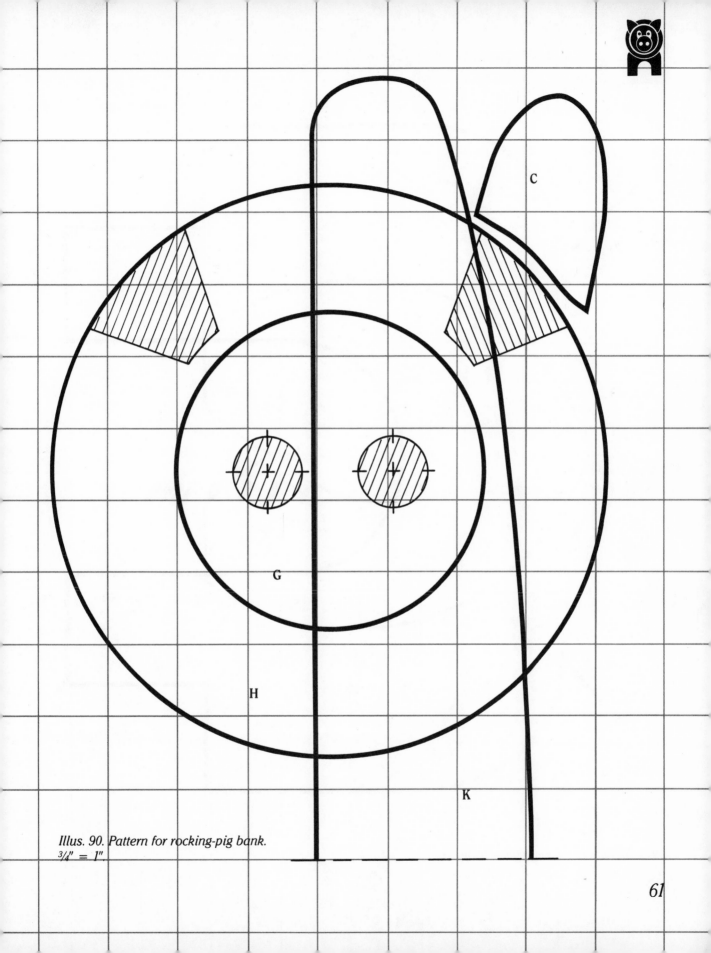

C

G

H

K

Illus. 90. Pattern for rocking-pig bank.
$^3/4'' = 1''$

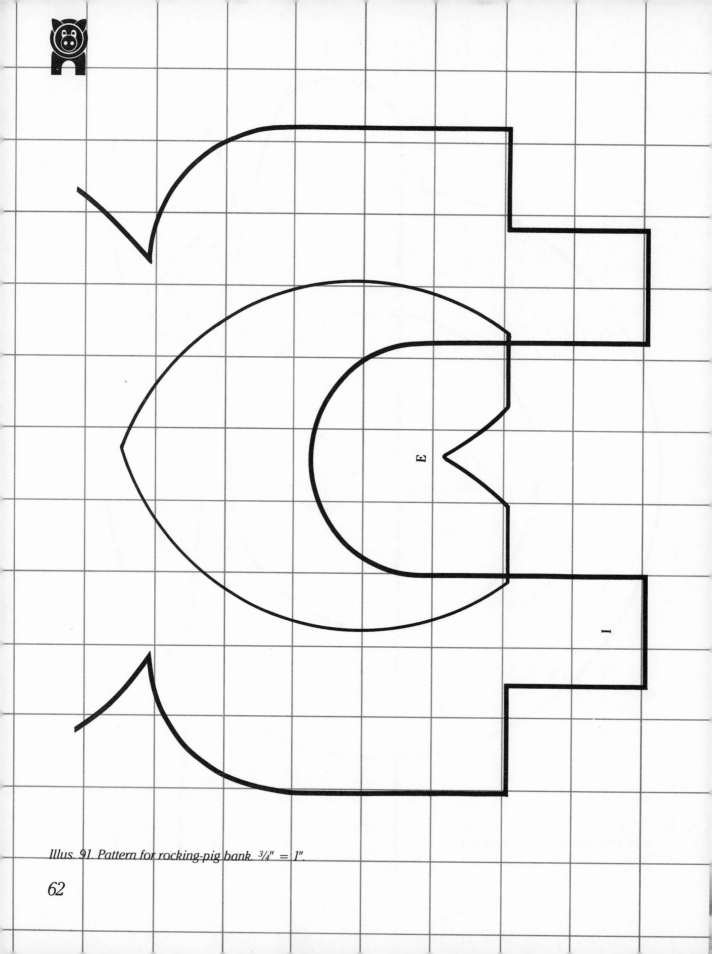

Illus. 91. Pattern for rocking-pig bank. ¾" = 1".

62

Illus. 92.

Watch the birdie!
You'll lose your composure
As the featherbrain
Hogs the exposure.

Camera

CAMERA

A simple lever pushes the vain birdie from his perch and he pivots down to peek into the lens. A quick twist of the knob and he's ready for the next shot. This plan includes a gag picture of— you guessed it—an upside-down birdie.

BODY

Cut a block of ¾ hardwood, 4″ × 3⅜″. Drill a 1″-dia. lens-hole as indicated on the pattern. Round all edges and sand. Cut (K) to shape, and from the leftover section mark and cut (C). Cut the ¼″ groove in (C). Glue and re-attach (C) to the camera body. Clamp and set aside to dry.

BIRDIE

Cut the bird body (D) from ¼ hardwood and sand. Mark and drill the ⅜″-dia. neck and axle holes as indicated on the pattern.

Use a ¾″-dia. wood ball for the head. Drill a ¼″-dia. beak-hole and a ⅜″-dia. neck-hole as indicated on the pattern.

Cut dowelling to length for the beak and make a small slit for the mouth. Glue and assemble the birdie.

MECHANISM

Cut a ¾″-dia. dowel to length for knob (I) and a ⅜″-dia. dowel to length for (J). Drill a shallow ⅜″-dia. hole ¾ of the way through the center of (I). Glue and assemble these pieces.

Unclamp the camera body when the glue has dried, and using the pattern side view (K), mark the location of the pivot hole in the side of the camera and drill a ⁷⁄₁₆″-dia. hole to a depth of 2¾″. Apply glue in the ⅜″-dia. hole in the birdie, and assemble.

LEVER

Using pattern (A), mark and cut out the lever and sand. Drill a ⁷⁄₃₂″-dia. hole in lever as indicated. Using pattern (C), mark the position of the lever pivot hole on the back of the camera body, then drill a ³⁄₁₆″-dia. hole, 1″ deep.

Cut ³⁄₁₆″-dia. dowel (B) to length. Position the lever and insert glued pivot dowel.

DECORATION

Use a woodburner to make the bird's eyes and to decorate the camera face. Finish as desired. Use pom-poms for bird's topknot and tail. Make photocopies of the upside-down birdie picture.

MATERIALS LIST

Ref.	No. of Pieces	Thickness in inches	Width in inches	Length in inches	Material
A	1	3/16	1/2	2½	black walnut
B	1		3/16 dia.	3/4	dowel
C	1	1¾	1¼	1⅝	maple
D	1	13/16	1¾	1¾	black walnut
E	2				pom-pom
F	1		3/8 dia.	1⅛	dowel
G	1		3/4 dia.		wooden ball
H	1		1/4 dia.	5/8	dowel
I	1		3/4 dia.	1/2	black walnut dowel
J	1		3/8 dia.	3	dowel
K	1	1¾	3⅜	4	maple

Illus. 93. "Snapshot" of birdie.

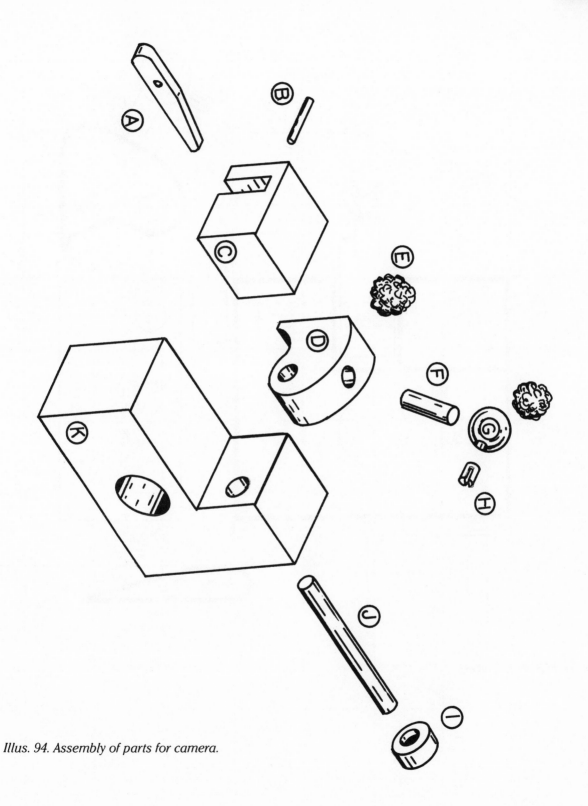

Illus. 94. Assembly of parts for camera.

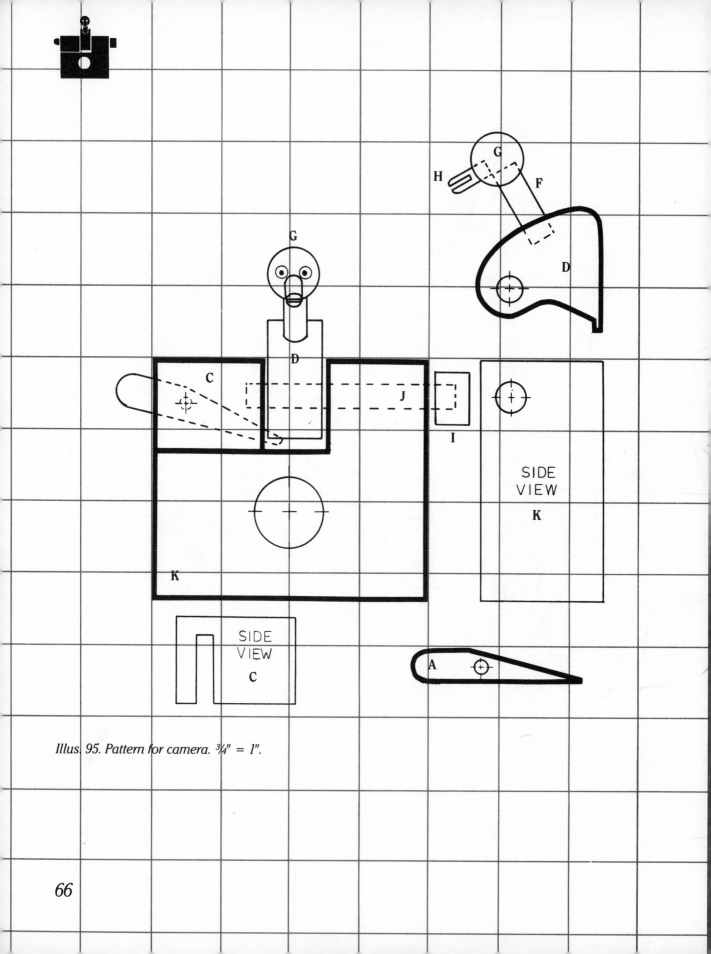

Illus. 95. Pattern for camera. ¾" = 1".

G

H G F

D

C D J

I

SIDE
VIEW
K

SIDE
VIEW
C

K

A

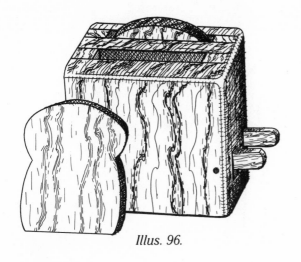

Illus. 96.

*You're cordially invited
To breakfast with toast:
I'll be your guest—
You be my host!*

Toaster

TOASTER

A lever is positioned beneath each slice of toast. A light touch of the lever raises the toast and a quick snap pops it into the air.

TOASTER HOUSING

Begin by cutting five layers (B) of 1 × 6 pine, 5″ long.

Using the pattern, mark and cut two of these pieces in the shape of a U. (Save the cut-out sections for the toast.)

Use the shaded area of pattern (A) to mark the notches on opposite sides of the two U-shaped pieces. (Refer to schematic.)

Notch both pieces to a depth of ⅜″. At this point, glue and clamp the five layers of the toaster body together and set aside to dry.

TOAST

Meanwhile, cut the toast from the cut-out sections of pine. Sand around the edges. Use a propane torch to darken the edges of the toast to simulate a crust. Sand the surfaces of the toast so that it will fit easily into its chambers.

LEVERS

Cut the levers (C) from hardwood, sand and drill a ⁷⁄₃₂″-dia. hole as indicated.

ASSEMBLY

Sand all surfaces flat, round edges, and finish sanding. Mark and drill ³⁄₁₆″-dia. holes in both sides of the toaster. Install the levers. Cut pivot pegs (D) and glue them into place.

MATERIALS LIST

Ref.	No. of Pieces	Thickness in inches	Width in inches	Length in inches	Material
A	2	¾	3½	4	pine
B	5	¾	5½	5	pine
C	2	⁵⁄₁₆	½	4¼	maple
D	2		³⁄₁₆ dia.	1½	dowel

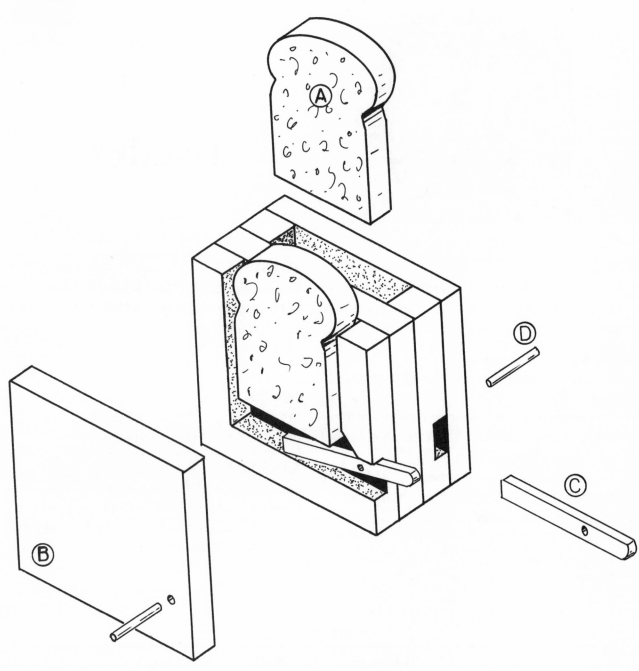

Illus. 97. Assembly of parts for toaster.

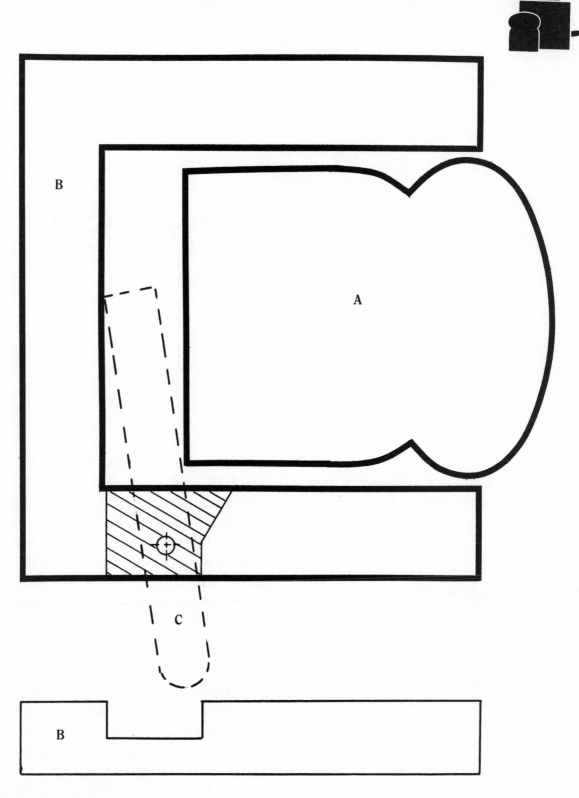

Illus. 98. Pattern for toaster. Full size.

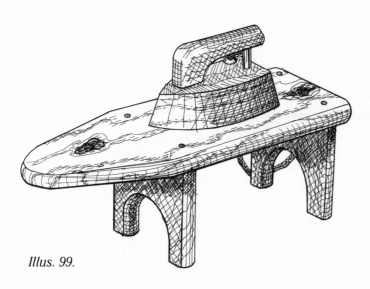

Illus. 99.

Iron out pressing problems
In trousers and skirts,
And life's little wrinkles
From blouses and shirts.

Iron Set

IRON SET

This is a quick and easy project. The iron is complete with steam vents.

BOARD TOP

From 1 × 6 pine, cut ironing board top to length. Using the pattern for (E), mark and cut the curve for the nose. Round the square corners. Now, round the top edges and sand.

LEGS

Using pattern (F), mark and cut the legs from ¼ hardwood. Round side edges and curve edges, but leave top and bottom edges flat. Sand, glue and attach legs to ironing board. While the glue is drying, begin working on the iron.

IRON

Mark out the iron handle (A) on ¼ hardwood and cut it out. Drill two ⅜"-dia. holes as indicated on pattern (A) and round all edges except the glue edge. Sand the iron handle. Glue dowels (B) and (C) into the iron handle.

Now use pattern (D) to mark out the iron base on 2 × pine. Cut out this piece with the bandsaw table set at 15°. Drill shallow ⅜"-dia. steam-vent holes. Use the iron handle as a guide to mark the position of the handle holes on the iron and drill with a ⅜" bit to a depth of ¾". Sand the iron and attach handle.

ASSEMBLY

Back to the ironing board—

Now that the glue has dried, drill ¼"-dia. holes and glue in pegs (I). To include a cord (optional), drill holes through the centers of two ½"-dia. screw-hole buttons, then thread them onto a cord and knot the cord ends. Drill a ½"-dia. hole (not all the way through) in the back legs and in the iron, and glue in the two buttons. (See Toy Safety Considerations.)

70

MATERIALS LIST

Ref.	No. of Pieces	Thickness in inches	Width in inches	Length in inches	Material
A	1	13/16	1¾	4¾	black walnut
B	1		⅜ dia.	1¾	dowel
C	1		⅜ dia.	1	dowel
D	1	1½	3¾	6⅜	pine
E	1	¾	5½	16	pine
F	2	13/16	5	4⅜	black walnut
G	1		3/16 dia.	18	cord
H	2		½ dia.		screw-hole buttons
I	4		¼ dia.	1½	dowel

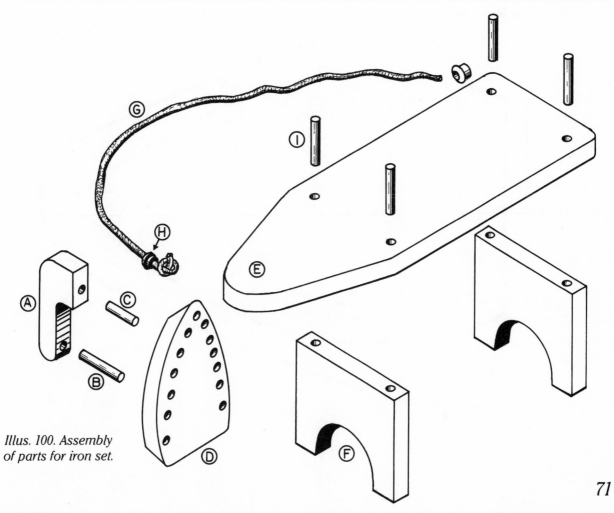

Illus. 100. Assembly of parts for iron set.

71

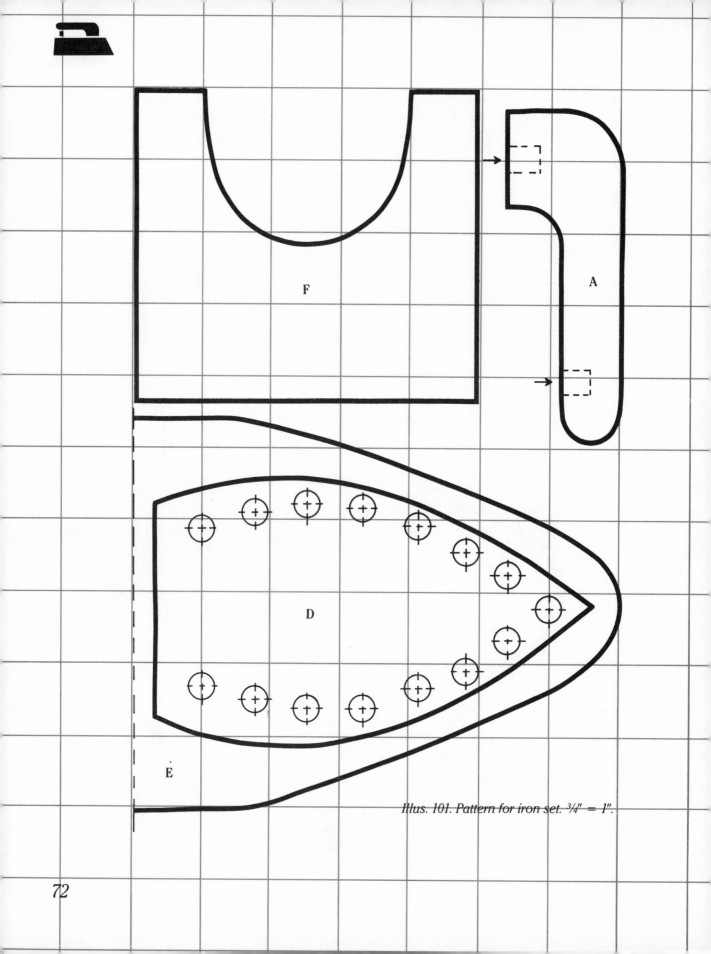

F

A

D

E

Illus. 101. Pattern for iron set. ¾″ = 1″.

72

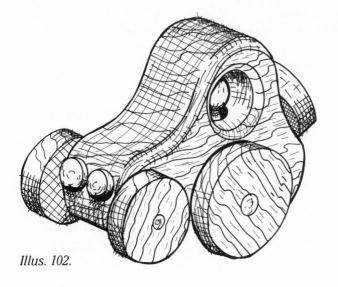

Illus. 102.

Jalopy bounces up and down
But the driver doesn't mind.
'Cause when the front end's in the air,
So is his behind!

Jalopy

JALOPY

Some drivers become so attached to their cars that they are oblivious to their faults. This old clunker, for example, clearly needs new shock absorbers and a wheel-balancing job. With each revolution of the wheels, the driver is pushed up by a peg in the rear axle. Off-center front wheels cause the front of the car to rise and fall.

CONSTRUCTION

Using the pattern, mark and cut the car body (D) from 8/4 hardwood. Drill the 1″-dia. window-hole as indicated on the pattern. Round all edges and sand.

Drill a ¹³⁄₁₆″-dia. hole for the driver in the position indicated by the arrow. Drill a ⁷⁄₁₆″-dia. rear-axle hole and a ⁵⁄₁₆″-dia. front-axle hole.

Drill shallow ½″-dia. holes in the front of the car for the button headlights.

Plug the center hole of two 1½″-dia. wheels and redrill the ¼″-dia. axle holes slightly off-center.

Cut ¼″-dia. and ⅜″-dia. dowels to length for axles. Cut ³⁄₁₆″-dia. dowel to length for axles. Cut driver to length. Drill a ³⁄₁₆″-dia. hole in the center of the rear axle.

ASSEMBLY

Before gluing the offset front wheels to the axle, make sure the wheels are in the same position. Insert driver and rear axle. Enlarge the axle holes in two 2″-dia. wheels to ⅜″ dia. and glue the rear wheels into position. Glue in axle peg and headlights. Drill a ⁷⁄₃₂″ hole in the back of the car, attach the spare tire, and secure it with a glued pivot peg.

MATERIALS LIST

Ref.	No. of Pieces	Thickness in inches	Width in inches	Length in inches	Material
A	3	½	1½ dia.		wheel
B	1		¼ dia.	2½	dowel
C	2		½ dia.		screw-hole buttons
D	1	1¾	3¼	4⅜	maple
E	1		¾ dia.	1¾	people turning
F	2	⁷⁄₁₆	2 dia.		wheel
G	1		³⁄₁₆ dia.	⅝	dowel
H	1		⅜ dia.	2¾	dowel
I	1		⁷⁄₃₂ dia.	1¼	peg

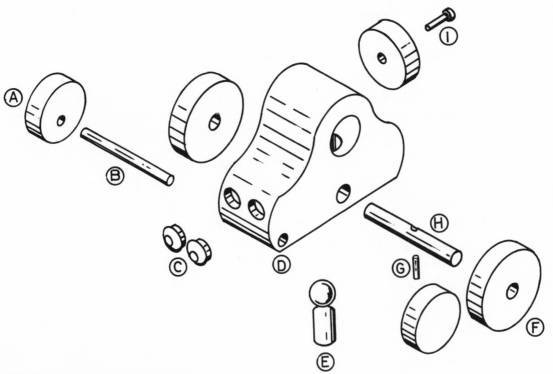

Illus. 103. Assembly of parts for jalopy.

74

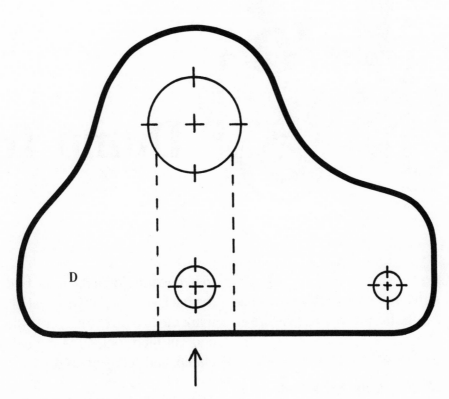

Illus. 104. Pattern for jalopy. Full size.

D

Trucking and dumping are lots of fun.
This stout wooden hauler can get the job done.

Dump Truck

Illus. 105.

DUMP TRUCK

The hinged bed is tripped by a lever mechanism and a peg in the front axle keeps the driver bouncing.

BODY

Using pattern (L), mark the truck body on a block of ⁴⁄₄ hardwood 4" wide by 6⅜" long. Drill a ¹³⁄₁₆"-dia. hole, 2½" deep for the trucker (arrow indicates the position). Now drill the 1"-dia. hole and cut out the truck body. Drill two ⁷⁄₁₆"-dia. axle holes and the ³⁄₁₆"-dia. hole for the bed-pivot dowel. Drill shallow ½"-dia. holes for the headlight buttons. Drill ⁵⁄₃₂"-dia. holes for the trip mechanism and the radiator cap. Using the back view of pattern (L), notch the body to accept the dump box. Round all edges except the grill, and sand.

BED

Using pattern (A), mark the dump-box bed on ⁴⁄₄ hardwood. Cut it out and drill the ⁷⁄₃₂"-dia. pivot hole as indicated on pattern (A). Sand inside surface of bed. Narrow the pivot tongue

to fit into the slot in the truck body as shown in the back view of pattern (A). Using pattern (B), mark the two box sides on ⅜"-thick hardwood and cut them out. Glue the sides to the box, clamp, and set aside to dry.

ASSEMBLY

Using pattern (E), mark the lever on a ¼"-thick piece of hardwood and cut it out. Drill a ³⁄₁₆"-dia. hole as indicated. Sand and attach lever to truck body with a glued ⁵⁄₃₂"-dia. pivot peg. Enlarge the holes in four 2"-dia. wheels to ⅜".

Cut two axles to length from ⅜"-dia. dowelling. Drill a ³⁄₁₆"-dia. hole in the center of the front axle. Cut the ³⁄₁₆"-dia. dowel (C) to length. Sand the assembled box and position it on the back of the truck. Glue and insert dowel (C). Put in the truck driver, insert the axles and glue on the wheels.

Cut the ³⁄₁₆"-dia. dowel for peg (G), round edges, and glue it into the front axle. Glue and insert ½"-dia. screw-hole plugs for headlights and a ⁵⁄₃₂"-dia. pivot peg for the radiator cap.

MATERIALS LIST

Ref.	No. of Pieces	Thickness in inches	Width in inches	Length in inches	Material
A	1	1¾	3¼	3¾	maple
B	2	⅜	2¾	3⅜	black walnut
C	1		³⁄₁₆ dia.	1¾	dowel
D	1		⁵⁄₃₂ dia.	¹³⁄₁₆	peg
E	1	¼	1¼	2	black walnut
F	4	⁷⁄₁₆	2 dia.		wheel
G	1		³⁄₁₆	⅝	dowel
H	2		⅜	2¾	dowel
I	1		¾ dia.	2⁵⁄₁₆	people turning
J	2		½ dia.		screw-hole button
K	1		⁵⁄₃₂ dia.	½	peg
L	1	1¾	4	6⅜	maple

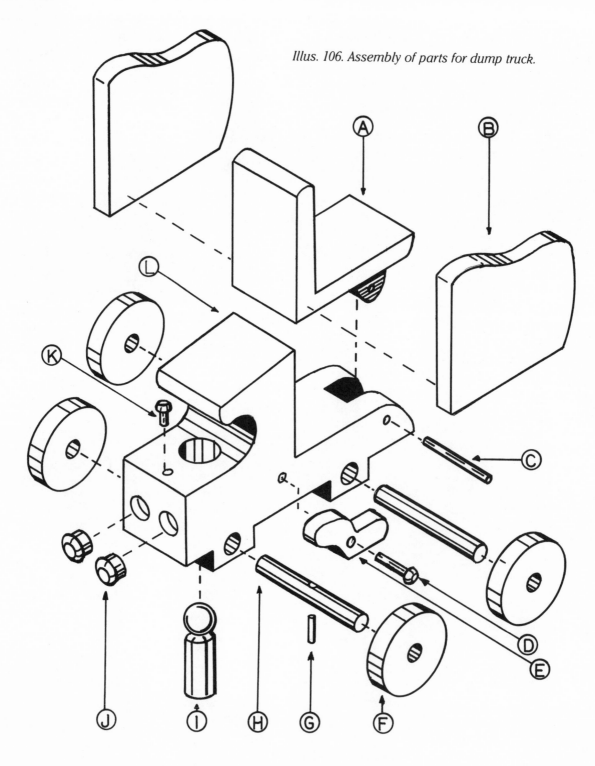

Illus. 106. Assembly of parts for dump truck.

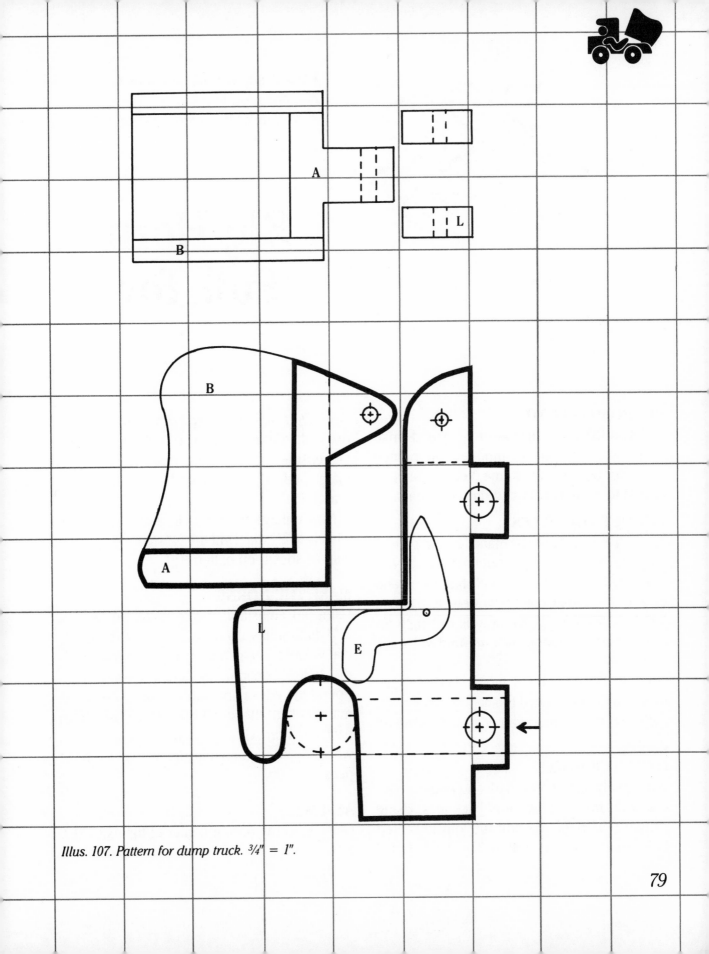

Illus. 107. Pattern for dump truck. ¾″ = 1″.

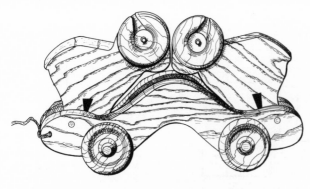

Illus. 108.

*When there are two would-be kings
And one mountain—
A meeting of the minds is imminent.*

Big Horn Pull Toy

BIG HORN PULL TOY

As it's pulled along, the rams rear up and strike their horns together. The hind legs are pinned and pivot between the frame pieces. Cams attached to each axle lift and drop the goats.

CUT OUT THE PIECES

To build this pull toy, first mark the goat pattern (A) on 2 × pine and cut out the bodies. Now mark the frame pieces (C) on ¼ hardwood and cut them out. Next, cut ⅜"-dia. dowels to length for axles (F). Cut ¼"-dia. dowels to length for (G). These will support the frame and will act as pivots.

Cams (F) are cut to length from ⅞"-dia. dowelling, then sanded to shape as shown on pattern (F). Now, round all edges and sand all pieces.

DRILL THE HOLES

Using body pattern (A), mark and drill the ⁵⁄₁₆"-dia. pivot holes in the rams' back legs. Using pattern (C), mark and drill the four indicated holes in each frame section. The 2 axle holes

are ⁷⁄₁₆" dia. and the 2 pivot dowel holes are ¼" dia. Drill ¼"-dia. holes in one end for pull cord. (To ensure that holes in both frame pieces match perfectly, clamp together and drill at one time.)

Now enlarge the holes in the four 2¼"-dia. wheels to ⅜" dia. Drill the ⅜"-dia. hole in each cam as shown on pattern (F).

MAKE THE HORNS

Using an adjustable circle cutter, make four 2¼"-dia. circles from ¼ hardwood (commercial wheels can also be used), and drill a ¾"-dia. hole ½" deep in the center of each circle. Round the edges and sand. Using pattern (B), mark and cut the small triangle sections from each ram horn. Glue the horns to the rams and, when dry, strengthen this joint with glued pivot pegs.

ASSEMBLY

Glue the cams on the center of the axles (E). Now, glue the ¼"-dia. dowels (G) into one side

of the frame and insert the assembled axles into the same side of the frame.

Position the ram bodies, facing each other, over these dowels.

Put a small amount of glue on the other end of dowels (G), and attach the opposite side of the frame. Make sure that the rams pivot freely between the frame pieces. Glue the wheels to the axles and attach the pull cord. (See Toy Safety Considerations.)

MATERIALS LIST

Ref.	No. of Pieces	Thickness in inches	Width in inches	Length in inches	Material
A	2	1½	6	6	pine*
B	4	¹³⁄₁₆	2¼ dia.		black walnut
C	2	¹³⁄₁₆	3⅜	12¾	black walnut
D	4	¹³⁄₁₆	2¼ dia.		birch
E	2		⅜ dia.	4¹⁵⁄₁₆	dowel
F	2		⅞ dia.	¾	dowel
G	2		¼ dia.	3¼	dowel
H	1				cord

*Body pieces should be made from lightweight wood, such as pine.

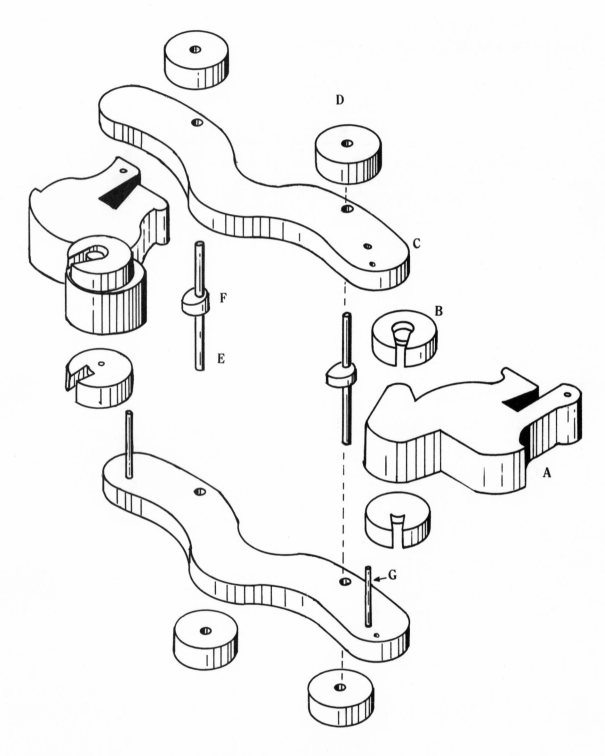

D

C

B

A

F

E

G

Illus. 109. Assembly of parts for big horn pull toy.

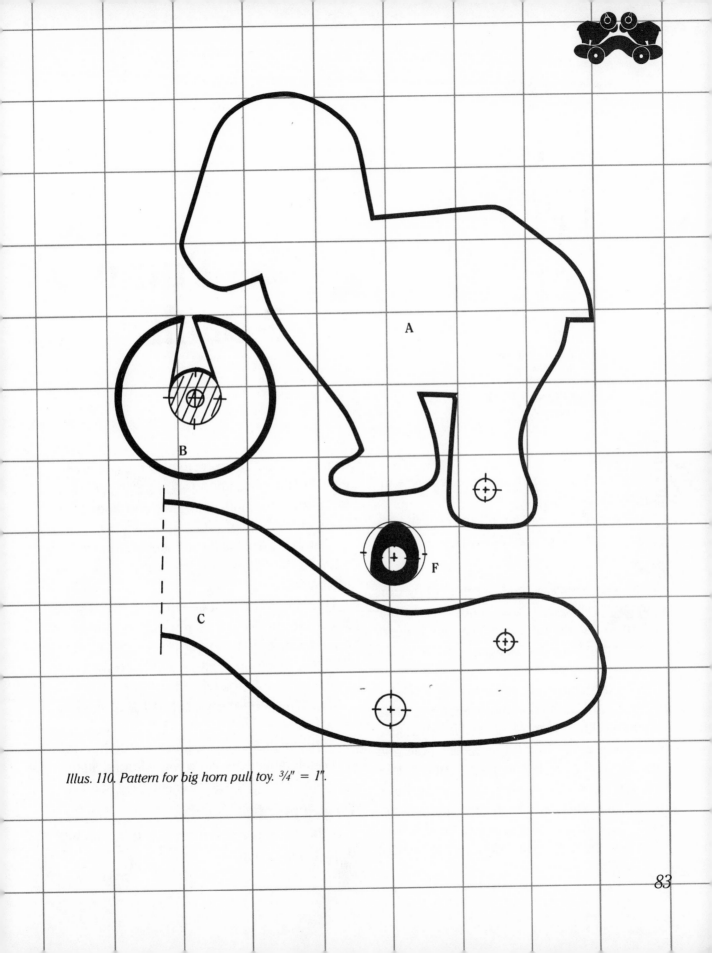

A

B

C

F

Illus. 110. Pattern for big horn pull toy. ³/₄" = 1".

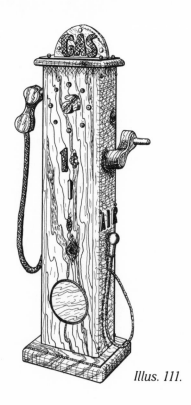

Illus. 111.

*Put in a coin
And turn the crank—
Hold the nozzle,
And fill the tank.*

Gas Pump Bank

GAS PUMP

As the crank is turned, the dial registers the purchase amount.

Pennies can be reclaimed through the circular door in the bottom of the pump.

BODY

Cut all four pieces of the gas-pump body (this plan fits nicely onto 1 × 12 pine). Use the dial pattern to locate and drill holes for the decorative buttons and the central $^{13}/_{16}$″-dia. arrow hole.

Make the coin slot by drilling two $^{7}/_{16}$″-dia. holes about 1″ apart and removing the remaining stock with a chisel or jigsaw. Use an adjustable circle cutter to cut the access hole and door. Reset the circle cutter, and cut the door from a scrap of pine. With the door in position, drill $^{1}/_{4}$″-dia. pivot holes from each side, extending 2″ through the sides and into the door.

Enlarge the holes in the door to $^{5}/_{16}$″ dia. Use a small section of dowel to plug the hole in the center of the door. Round and sand the edges of the door, hole and coin slot, and attach the door with $^{1}/_{4}$″-dia. dowel pegs.

Clamp the front and back sections and drill a $^{13}/_{16}$″-dia. hole through the front and $^{1}/_{2}$″-dia. into the back.

Drill all indicated holes in the body pieces. Note that the $^{3}/_{8}$″-dia. screw-button holes are drilled only $^{1}/_{2}$″ into the side pieces, and that the $^{13}/_{16}$″-dia. crank-hole extends through the right side and $^{1}/_{2}$″ into the left side.

Round around the outside edge of the gas nozzle hole.

Glue and assemble the four sides of the body by countersinking wood screws. Round all but top and bottom edges, glue and then sand.

OTHER PIECES

Use the same pattern to cut nozzle and crank from ⁸⁄₄ hardwood.

Use side view to mark and cut nozzle to shape.

Drill ¾″-dia. holes in the nozzle and crank. Drill ⅝″-dia. hole in the nozzle to accept the cord. Round the edges, and sand.

Cut indicated lengths of ¾″-dia. dowel for nozzle, crank and dial. Round one end of the nozzle dowel and one end of the handle, and glue them into place. Using pattern (B), cut arrow indicator from ¼ hardwood. Drill a ¾″-dia. hole, as indicated, in arrow. Sand.

Use an adjustable circle cutter to cut two 5″-dia. and one 2½″-dia. pulley circles. Glue and clamp the circles together and set the pulley aside to try.

AIR NOZZLE

Drill a shallow hole in a wooden ball or drawer pull to accept a length of ¾″-dia. dowel. A ⅜″-dia. hole is drilled into the end of the dowel to attach the cord, and another ⅜″-dia. hole in the ball serves as an "air outlet" and hanger. (The air nozzle plugs onto a small length of ⅜″-dia. dowel glued in the hole in the gas-pump body.)

ASSEMBLY

Glue ¾″-dia. dowels into crank and indicator, and mark placement of ¼″-dia. retainer peg holes, then drill. (See inset drawing.) Drill a ¾″-dia. hole through the center of the pulley.

Put crank, indicator and pulley into gas pump. Make sure that the rubber band (#107—

7″ long × ⅝″ wide × 1⁄16″ thick) is in place. Then secure with glued dowel peg.

Pulleys are glued to dowel. Lock unit in place with glued dowel peg.

Cut the sign and the top plate from 1 × pine. Use the pattern to mark and drill ½″ holes in the sign for decorative buttons.

Cut the base from 2 × pine. Round the edges of all three of these parts (bottom edges of base and top, and glue edge of sign are *not* rounded) and then sand.

Glue and attach the sign to the top plate and strengthen with wood screws, countersunk ½″. Glue and attach the top and strengthen this joint by countersinking wood screws.

Heat and attach the nylon cords to the nozzles. Thread the other ends through the pump body and knot them. Cut the letters from ¼″-thick hardwood, sand, and glue into position. Glue in decorative buttons around the dial, and buttons or dowel plugs for screw-hole covers.

Illus. 113. Assemble the gas pump body with woodscrews and cover the holes with decorative buttons.

Illus. 112. Use a small length of dowel to hold the crank and arrow shafts in place.

Illus. 114. Route a decorative bead around one surface of the top and base plates.

MATERIALS LIST

Ref.	No. of Pieces	Thickness in inches	Width in inches	Length in inches	Material
A	1	¾	6	32	pine
B	1	¾	5	32	pine
C	1	¾	6	32	pine
D	1	¾	5	32	pine
E	1	¾	5 dia.		pine
F	1	¾	2¼	2½	black walnut
G	1	1¾	2¼	5⅞	maple
H	1		¾ dia.	3½	dowel
I	2	¾	5 dia.		pine
J	1	¾	2½ dia.		pine
K	1		¾ dia.	8⅛	dowel
L	1	1¾	2¼	2½	black walnut
M	1		¾ dia.	2¾	dowel
N	1	¾	4	7½	pine
O	1	¾	6½	9¼	pine
P	1	1¾	9¼	11	pine
Q	1		1¼ dia.		wooden ball
R	1		¾ dia.	1½	dowel
S	1		¾ dia.	5⅜	dowel
T	1		⅝ dia.	36	cord
U	1				#107 rubber band
V	1		3/16 dia.	24	cord
W	1		⅜ dia.	1	dowel
X			¼ dia.	2	dowel

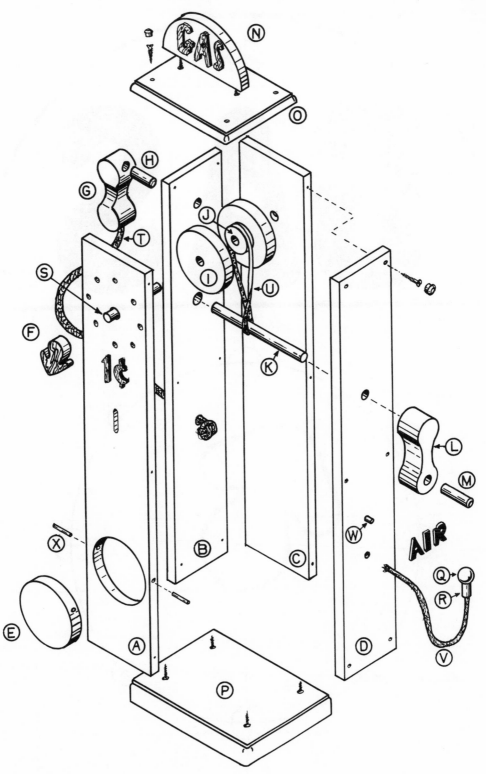

Illus. 115. Assembly of parts for gas pump bank.

Illus. 116. Pattern for gas pump bank. ¾" = 1".

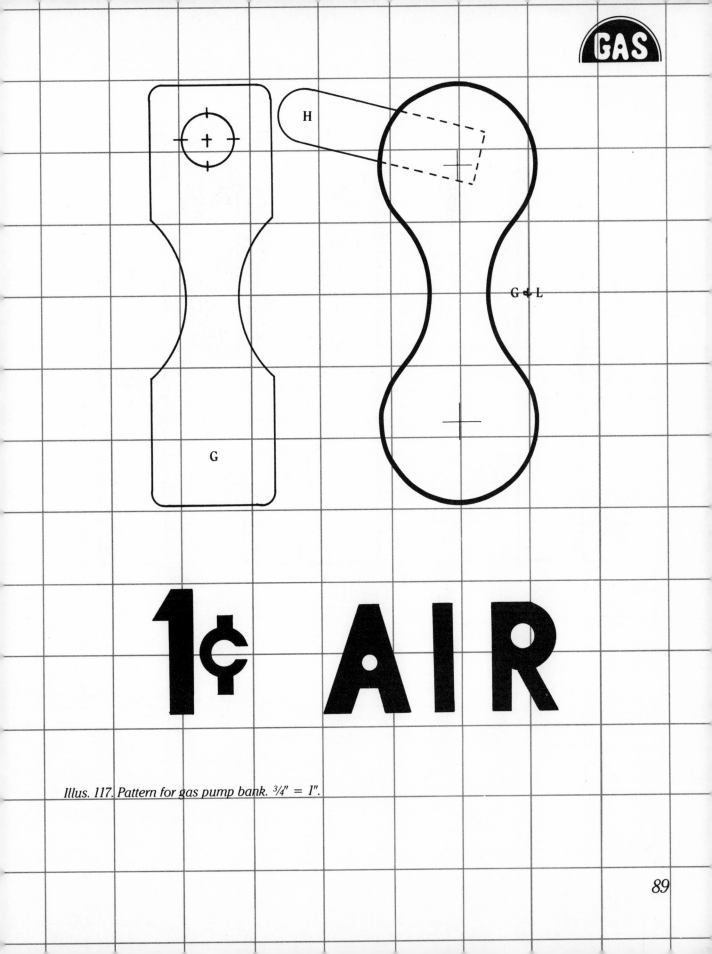

Illus. 117. Pattern for gas pump bank. ¾" = 1".

89

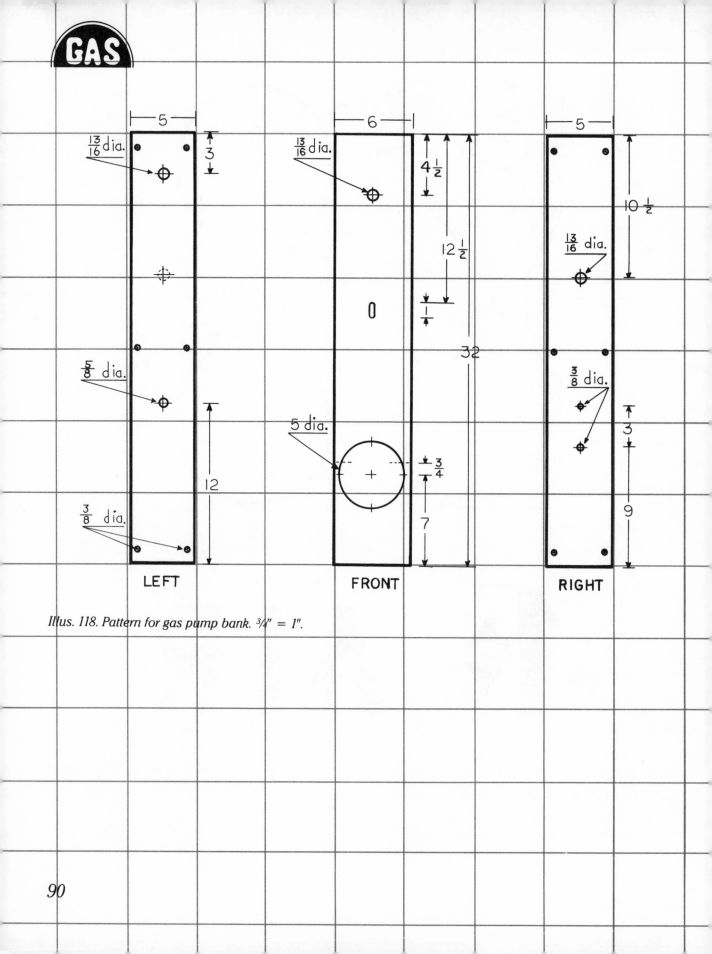

GAS

$\frac{13}{16}$ dia.

5

3

$\frac{5}{8}$ dia.

12

$\frac{3}{8}$ dia.

LEFT

$\frac{13}{16}$ dia.

6

$4\frac{1}{2}$

$12\frac{1}{2}$

0

1

32

5 dia.

$\frac{3}{4}$

7

FRONT

5

$10\frac{1}{2}$

$\frac{13}{16}$ dia.

$\frac{3}{8}$ dia.

3

9

RIGHT

Illus. 118. Pattern for gas pump bank. ¾" = 1".

Illus. 119.

A robot that swings its arms
And moves its lips
Without the use of batteries
Or micro-chips.

Robot

ROBOT

A child's imagination and gentle push is enough to march this wood robot through any adventure. The top of its head is attached to a dowel which extends through the body. A peg in the axle lifts this dowel to open the mouth. The robot's arms pivot from the shoulders and are pushed by an off-center peg in each wheel. Although there are a number of pieces and steps to this plan, it is a relatively easy toy to build.

BODY

Using pattern (O), mark and cut out the body from ¾ hardwood.

For a decorated chest, drill six shallow holes ⅜″-dia. and glue in short lengths of dowel or screw-hole plugs. Round the edges and sand the body. Center and drill a 1″-dia. hole ½″ deep in the bottom of the body. Cut a ⅝″ length of 1″ dowel (H) and glue it into the hole. This dowel will allow for easy alignment and a strong glue joint between the body and base, and should extend ⅛″. Drill a ⁷⁄₁₆″-dia. hole through the center of this dowel and through the robot body. Drill ¼″-dia. armholes in the body as shown on side-view pattern (O).

ARMS

Now, using pattern (F), mark and cut two arm pieces from ½″-thick hardwood. Drill a shallow ⁹⁄₁₆″-dia. hole in each arm as indicated on pattern (F). Drill a ⁵⁄₁₆″-dia. hole through the center of each of these holes. Sand the arms.

HEAD

The head is a single block of ¾ hardwood, 2″ wide and 2″ long. Using the pattern, mark the location of the eyes and nose and drill shallow ⅜″-dia. holes. Using side-view pattern (B), locate and drill ¼″-dia. holes for ear pegs. Locate the top center of head (B) and drill a ¼″-dia. hole all the way through. Round all edges and sand. Then, using side-view pattern (B), cut the jaw (E) from the head block. Enlarge the hole in (E) to ⁷⁄₁₆″-dia. Enlarge the hole in the bottom of (B) to ⅜″-dia. to a depth of ⅝″.

BASE

Using side-view pattern (L), mark and cut the base from ¾ hardwood. Round the edges and sand. Center, and, using a Forstner bit, drill a 1" hole nearly to the bottom of (L). Locate and drill a $\frac{7}{16}$"-dia. hole as shown on side-view pattern (L). Cut a $\frac{3}{8}$"-dia. dowel to length for axle (M). Drill a $\frac{3}{16}$"-dia. hole through the center of the axle as shown in the schematic drawing. Enlarge the center hole in two $1\frac{1}{2}$"-dia. wheels for axle (M). Drill $\frac{1}{4}$"-dia. holes in wheels for pegs (J) slightly off-center.

ASSEMBLY

Cut dowel (D) to length and glue it to head (B). Glue and insert pivot pegs for antennae and ears and $\frac{3}{8}$" screw-hole button for nose. With the holes aligned, glue the jaw (E) to the body (O) and set these parts aside to dry. Now begin assembling the base. Insert axle (M) in base (L) and glue on wheels. (Note: Position wheels so that pegs (J) will move arms alternately.) Cut $\frac{1}{4}$"-dia. dowel pegs (J) to length and glue them into the holes in the wheels. Cut $\frac{3}{16}$"-dia. dowel (N) to length, round the ends and glue into the hole in the center of the axle.

HEAD, BODY AND BASE ASSEMBLY

Cut the $\frac{3}{4}$"-dia. dowel (I) to length and drill a $\frac{3}{8}$"-dia. hole in its center. Position the head on the body unit and secure it by gluing dowel (I) flush with the bottom of dowel (D). Making certain that the arms swing freely, attach them to the body with glued pivot pegs. Dry-fit the body to the base, checking to make sure that the movement is satisfactory. Then glue these two pieces together.

MATERIALS LIST

Ref.	No. of Pieces	Thickness in inches	Width in inches	Length in inches	Material
A	5		$\frac{1}{4}$ dia.		turned pegs
B	1	$1\frac{3}{4}$	2	2	maple
C	1		$\frac{3}{8}$ dia.		screw-hole button
D	1		$\frac{3}{8}$ dia.	4	dowel
E	(see B above)				
F	2	$\frac{1}{2}$	$\frac{3}{4}$	$3\frac{3}{8}$	maple
G	6		$\frac{3}{8}$ dia.	$\frac{1}{4}$	dowel
H	1		1 dia.	$\frac{5}{8}$	dowel
I	1		$\frac{3}{4}$ dia.	$\frac{1}{4}$	dowel
J	2		$\frac{1}{4}$ dia.	$\frac{3}{4}$	dowel
K	2	$\frac{1}{2}$	$1\frac{1}{2}$ dia.		wheel
L	1	$1\frac{1}{2}$	2	$2\frac{1}{2}$	maple
M	1		$\frac{3}{8}$ dia.	$3\frac{1}{8}$	dowel
N	1		$\frac{3}{16}$ dia.	$\frac{3}{4}$	dowel
O	1	$1\frac{3}{4}$	$2\frac{1}{4}$	3	maple

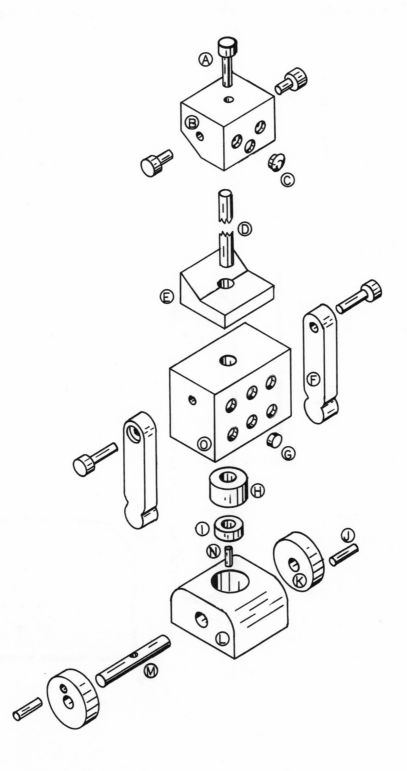

Illus. 120. Assembly of parts for robot.

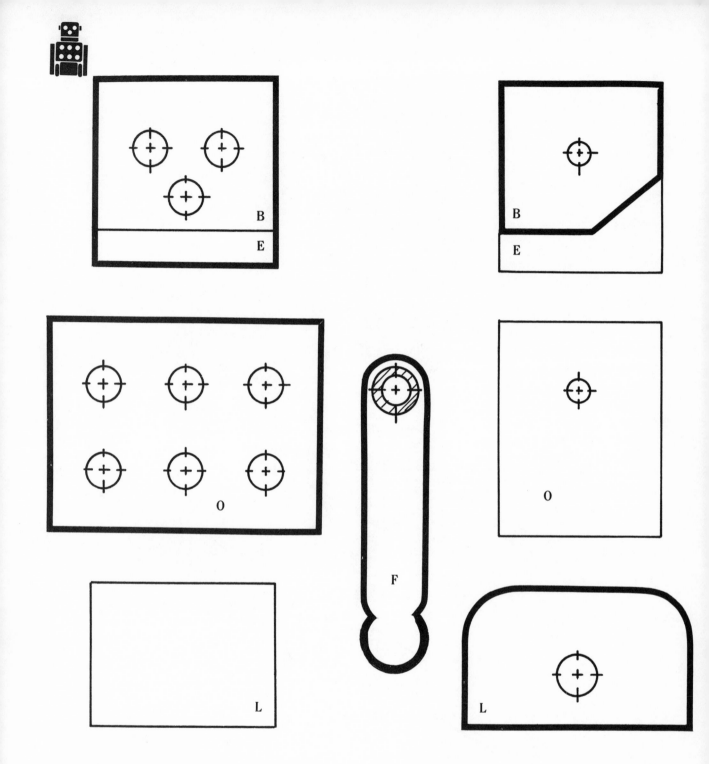

Illus. 121. Pattern for robot. Full size.

Illus. 122. Back view of robot.

Illus. 123.

You think, Mr. Jones, it's your sweat that
Makes us roll?
Well, let me control the throttle,
You come back and shovel coal!

Big Train

TRAIN

Trains are favorites among woodworkers. This is a colorful, three-piece version of a classic steam train. The set includes a group of whimsical figures and a surprise mechanism that causes the coal man to revolve as if stoking the engine's firebox.

ENGINE

Part of the engine is made from ½"-thick pine. Begin by cutting out these pieces (B,C,D,E), using the dimensions indicated on the materials list. Use the pattern to mark the arched windows of the cab and then cut them out. Round around the window edges.

The roof of the cab (A) is made of 1x pine. Cut it to size, round the top edge, and sand all pieces. Now, assemble the cab. (Painting and staining should be done prior to assembly) by gluing and clamping or using small nails.

Glue up two pieces of 2 × pine to make the required 3" thickness for (F). When dry, use pattern (F) to cut to size. Sand and attach to (E). Glue and attach cab to (F). Use pattern (G) to cut the coupler from 1 × pine. Drill a ⁷⁄₁₆"-dia. hole as indicated. Sand, glue, and attach to (E). Now, drill a ⁹⁄₁₆"-dia. axle hole as indicated, and sand. Then, glue and attach one block 1½" from the front of (E) and the second 1" away from the first.

COW CATCHER

To make the cow catcher (K), glue up a blank, using a piece of 1 × pine and a piece of 2 × pine. Trace the cow-catcher pattern on this blank and cut it out with the bandsaw table set at 40°. Sand the cow catcher and attach to (E).

Cut the wheels (J, I) from 1x pine using an adjustable circle cutter. Enlarge the center holes to ½"-dia. and sand. Cut axles (T) and (S) to length, and glue and attach wheels to train.

TURNINGS

Use the patterns as guides to make the six turnings (L,M,N,O,R). Sand while each piece is still on the lathe. Drill the indicated holes in the boiler. Attach the boiler to the base (E) with wood screws.

To make the lantern, cut block (Q) and drill a shallow ¾"-dia. hole in the front, and a ¼"-dia. hole in the bottom. Sand turning (R) to shape, and glue to the top of (Q). Glue and attach lantern, smokestack, and whistle to boiler.

Drill a ¾"-dia. hole nearly all the way through the center of each (L). Attach them to platform (E) using ¼"-dia. dowel pins. Position it so that the back of the cylinders are 4¼" from the front of the platform.

Use pattern to cut (P) from ⅜"-thick hardwood. Drill a pivot hole in (P) for a countersunk wood screw. Assemble.

ENGINE MATERIALS LIST

Ref.	No. of Pieces	Thickness in inches	Width in inches	Length in inches	Material
A	1	¾	5½	8	pine
B	2	½	6½	5½	pine
C	1	½	4	6½	pine
D	1	½	5	5½	pine
E	1	½	3	12½	pine
F	1	3	3	7	pine
G	1	¾	3	4¾	pine
H	2	1½	2¼	2½	pine
I	4	¾	3 dia.		pine
J	2	¾	6 dia.		pine
K	1	2¼	3⅛	6½	pine
L	2		1¾ dia.	3	pine
M	1		4 dia.	8	pine
N	1		3 dia.	5¼	pine
O	1		1¾ dia.	2½	pine
P	2	⅜	¾	9¼	maple
Q	1	¾	1	1½	pine
R	1	⅝	1⅝ dia.		pine
S	1		½	4¾	dowel
T	2		½ dia.	3⅛	dowel

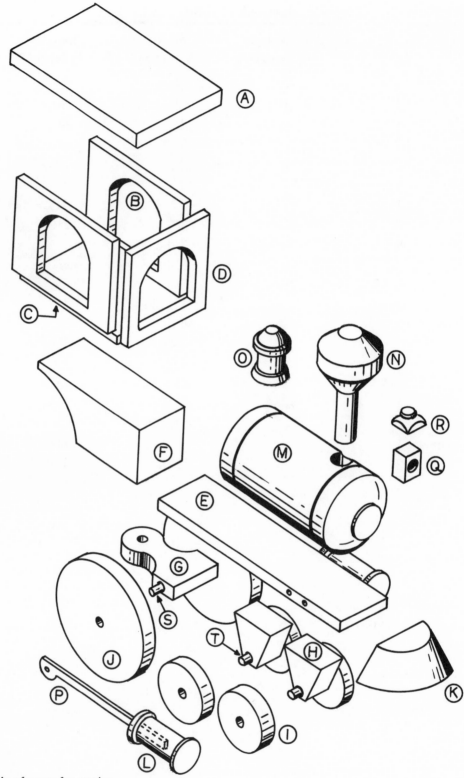

Illus. 124. Assembly of parts for engine.

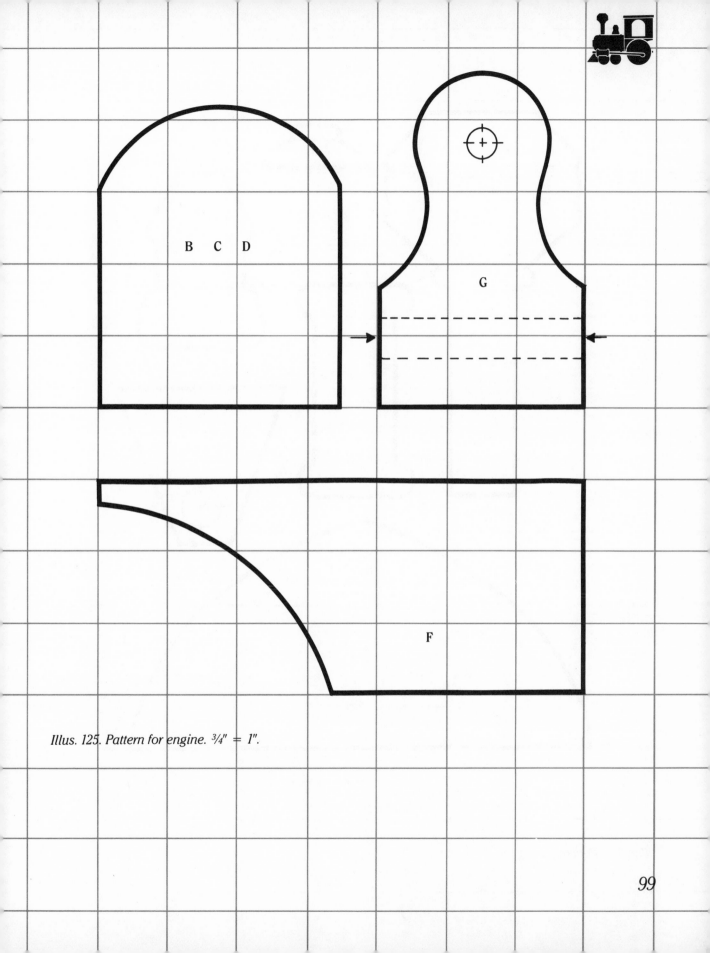

B C D

G

F

Illus. 125. Pattern for engine. ³/₄″ = 1″.

99

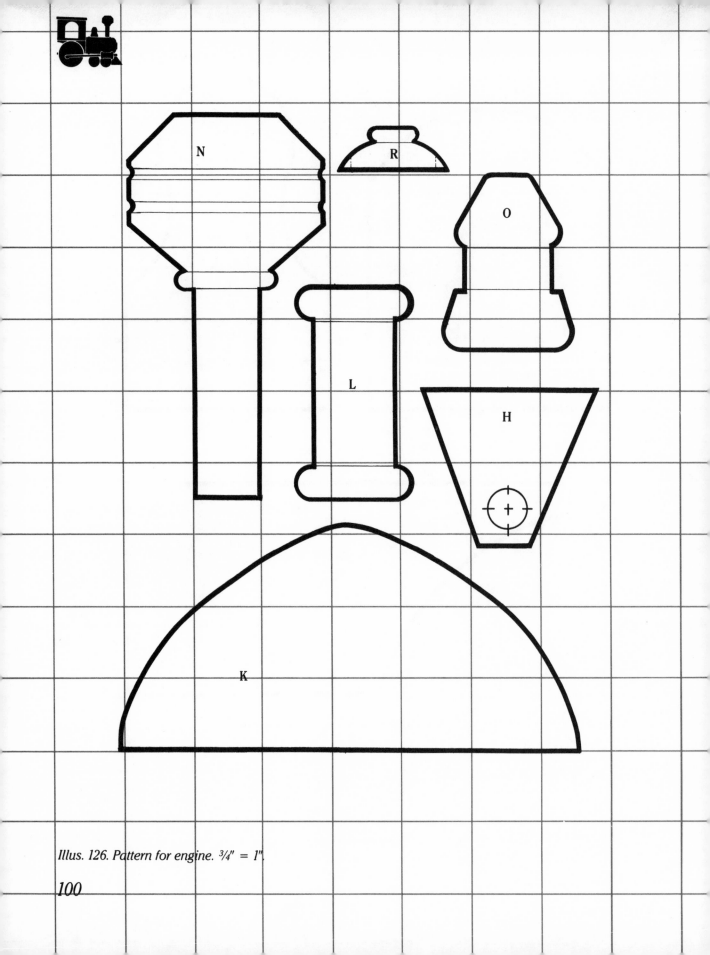

Illus. 126. Pattern for engine. ¾" = 1".

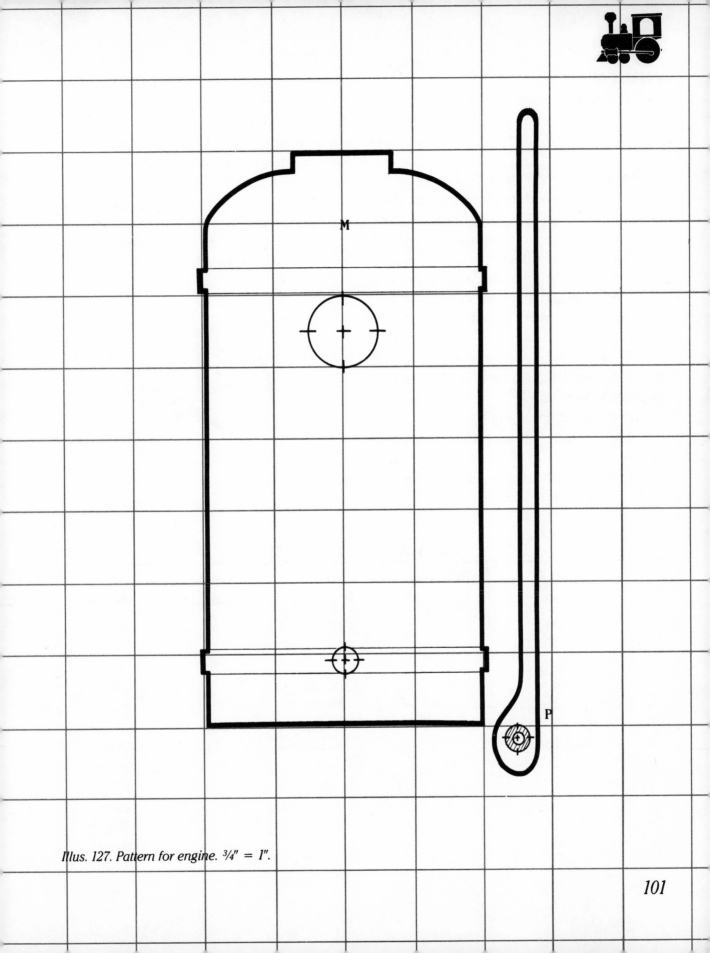

M

P

Illus. 127. Pattern for engine. ¾" = 1".

101

COAL CAR

First use pattern (A) to cut the bottom of the coal car from 1x pine. Then, from ½″ pine cut the two car sides (C) and the car front (B). Sand all pieces.

Glue and assemble the car sides to the car bottom. (Painting and staining should be done prior to assembly.) Glue up a block for piece (E). Use pattern (C) to mark and then cut out (E). Sand and glue (E) into the car.

To house the mechanism, drill a 1⅜″-dia. hole 1½″ deep and 4½″ from the front of (A). Drill this hole the rest of the way through with a 9/16″ bit.

Drill the two 9/16″-dia. axle holes. (Front-axle hole is centered through the middle of the 1⅜″-dia. mechanism hole.)

Drill the ⅜″ connector holes.

Cut ⅜″-dia. dowels to length for (G) and glue and assemble.

Cut ½″ dowel (K) to length. Cut the wheels (I, J, L).

Glue and attach wheels (L) to (K) and position this assembly in (E). Now glue wheel (J) to the other end of (K).

Use an adjustable circle cutter to cut out the 4½″-dia. wheels, and sand. Cut two axles (F) to length. Position axles in the car, making certain that wheel (I) is slightly off-set (see insert mechanism drawing), and glue on the wheels.

Cut block (H) to size and glue on pieces of irregularly sanded wood to simulate coal.

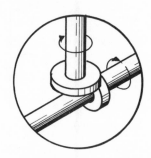

Illus. 128. The wheel attached to the coal car's axle turns the wheel attached to the coal man.

COAL CAR MATERIALS LIST

Ref.	No. of Pieces	Thickness in inches	Width in inches	Length in inches	Material
A	1	¾	2¾	16	pine
B	1	½	3¾	4¾	pine
C	2	½	5½	8¾	pine
D	4	¾	4½ dia.		pine
E	1	2¾	2¾	9	pine
F	2		½ dia.	5⅜	dowel
G	2		⅜ dia.	1¼	dowel
H	1	1½	2¾	3⅝	pine
I	1	¼	1 dia.		wheel
J	1	¼	1¼ dia.		pine
K	1		½ dia.	6	dowel
L	2	½	1¾		wheel

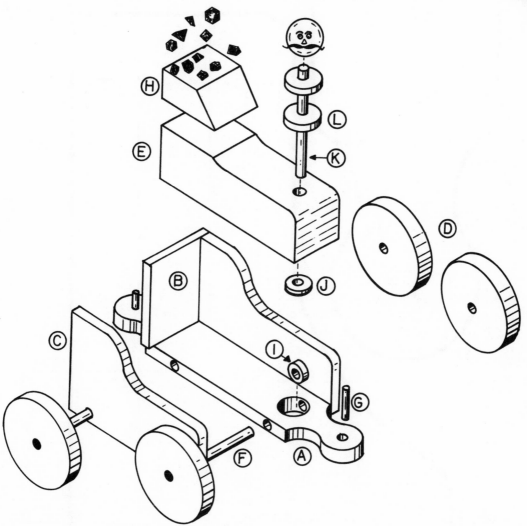

Illus. 129. Assembly of parts for the coal car.

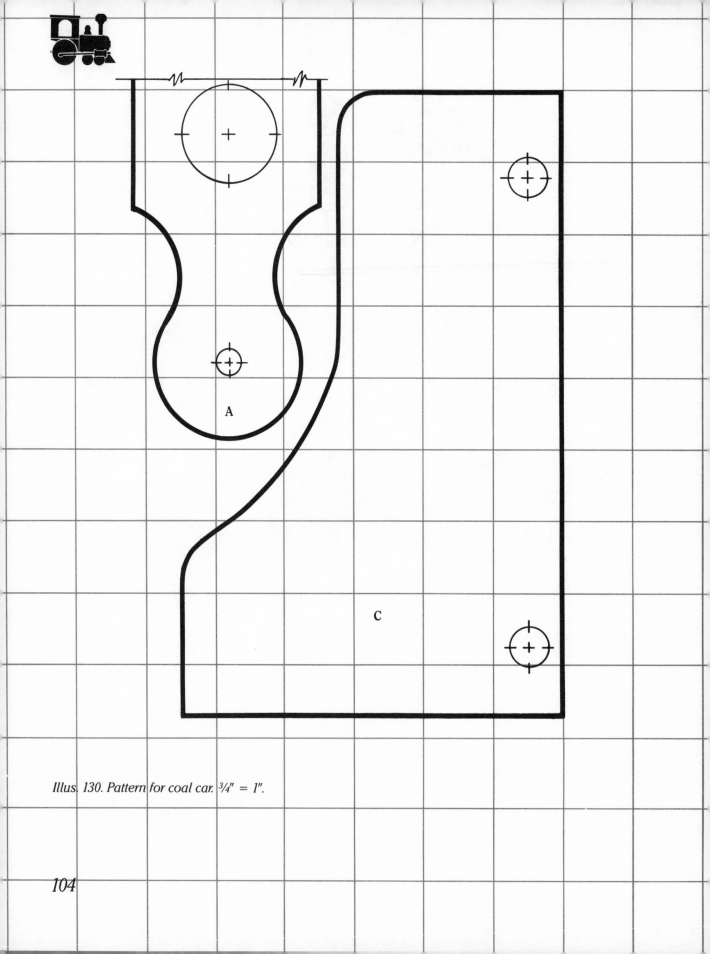

A

C

Illus. 130. Pattern for coal car. ³⁄₄″ = 1″.

CABOOSE

Begin by cutting the car bottom (A) from 1 × pine. Then cut the ½″ pine walls and floor (B, C, D). Using a coping saw or jigsaw to cut out the windows.

Use pattern (B) and (C) to mark and cut roof sections (H) and (J) from ½″ pine. Cut roof section (I) from 1 × pine.

Using pattern (E), cut 2 end rails. Using pattern (F) cut two wheel blocks and drill the 9/16″-dia. axle holes.

Sand all pieces and glue and assemble. (Painting and staining should be done prior to assembly.)

Drill a ½″-dia. hole in the top of the caboose. Cut, glue in dowel (K). Cut two axles (L). Using an adjustable circle cutter cut out the four 3″-dia. wheels and sand. Position axles in wheel holders and glue on wheels.

CABOOSE MATERIALS LIST

Ref.	No. of Pieces	Thickness in inches	Width in inches	Length in inches	Material
A	1	¾	3	12	pine
B	2	½	5	6	pine
C	2	½	3	5½	pine
D	1	½	3	5	pine
E	2	½	2¼	3	pine
F	2	1½	1⅞	3	pine
G	4	¾	3 dia.		pine
H	1	½	4½	8	pine
I	1	¾	1½	3	pine
J	1	½	2¾	4½	pine
K	1		½ dia.	1½	dowel
L	2		½ dia.	4½	dowel

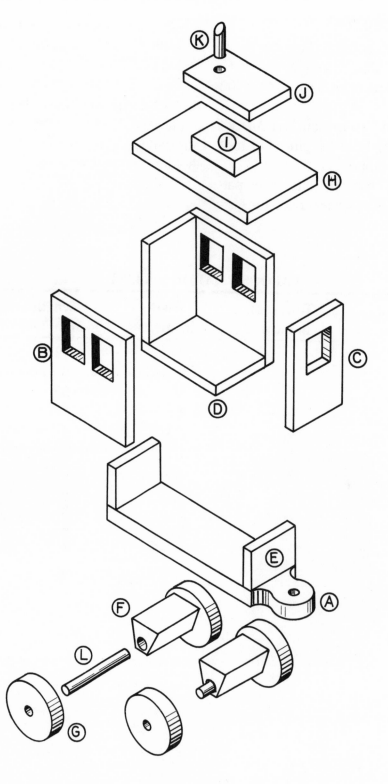

Illus. 131. Assembly of parts for caboose.

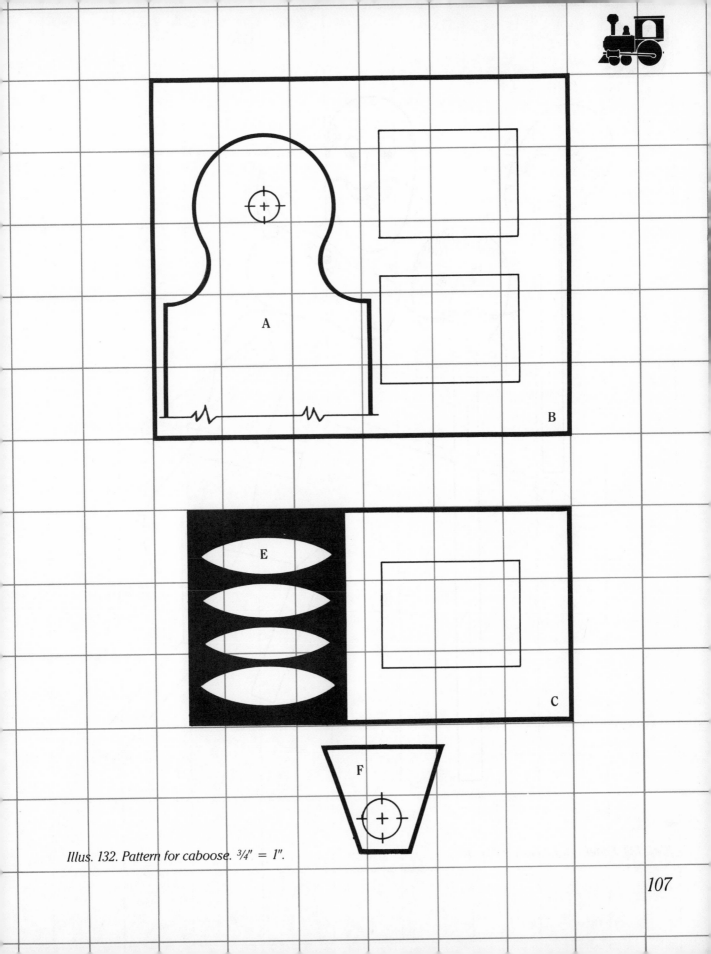

Illus. 132. Pattern for caboose. ³⁄₄″ = 1″.

107

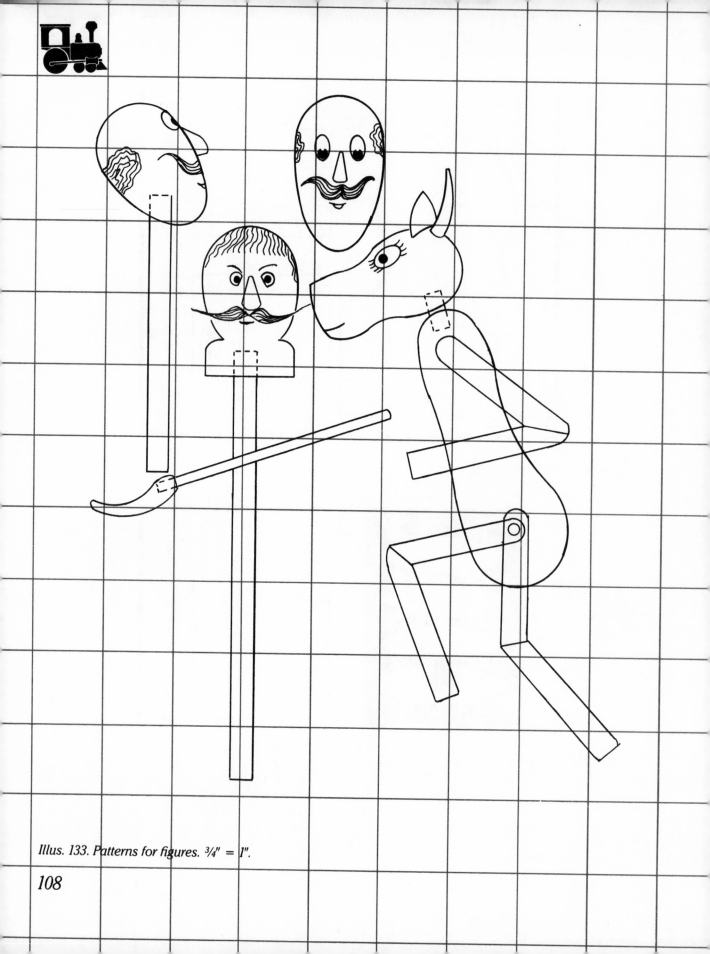

Illus. 133. Patterns for figures. ¾″ = 1″.

3
COMMERCIAL
TOYMAKING

Selling Toys

Rosemary pleaded with her husband, "Scott, you've got to put away that paperwork and come to bed. Remember you have to go to work in the morning."

"If this plan works," replied Scott, "I may never have to go to work again. Listen to this. It's a plan for turning my toymaking hobby into a full-time business. First, I quit my job . . ."

"I don't like it already," muttered Rosemary.

". . . Then, I put my four best toy plans into production. It takes an average of 18 minutes to make one of my toys. If I sell each toy for $6.50, I can make $21.67 per hour. If I work 18 hours a day, I could bring in $390 easy—that's $1,950 per week, or $7,800 per month and $93,600 per year. WOW! That's more than the President makes!"

Rosemary pulled the covers over her head, closed her eyes, and hoped that Scott would come to his senses before morning.

When starting a toy business, it is easy to be carried away on a wave of enthusiasm. Before tendering your job resignation, though, you should know that it takes just as much time and effort to sell toys as to build them. A number of questions arise about selling wooden toys:

Q. Where do I start?
A. First, a word of warning. As with any business venture, it is wise to seek the advice of profes-sionals before becoming too deeply involved. You will, at some point, want to see a lawyer, an accountant and an insurance representative. You need to find out about state and local licensing requirements as well as about taxation obligations. You need to keep excellent records and you should have liability insurance. With this said, the first step is to consider your options.

Q. What are my options?
A. Basically, you have two: To sell your toys wholesale or to sell them retail. Selling toys retail usually means that you will be selling one toy at a time, directly to the consumer who will pay you a retail price. Wholesaling, on the other hand, involves selling in quantity to a retail store owner, who will, in turn sell your toys to the consumer. You will receive approximately one half of the retail price.

Q. How can I sell my toys retail?
A. Some sales are usually made by word of mouth alone. Relatives, friends, and neighbors may see your toys and wish to buy them. If you want to sell to people outside this circle, how-ever, you will need some method of exposing your toys to the general public. One of the best and most popular methods is to display them at a weekend street market. Here craftspeople are brought together in a festive atmosphere to sell

their handiwork. For a percentage of the profit (usually about 10%) or a set fee, a vendor is provided with space to set up a booth. This is an attractive way to reach a lot of people.

If you have a large amount of money to invest, you may wish to open your own retail store. Shelves could be stocked with your toys alone or might include products or other craftspeople. Another alternative is to sell your toys through mail-order by placing ads in magazines. You should be aware that these two alternatives involve a high degree of risk and require careful study and planning.

Q. How can I sell my toys wholesale?
A. You could take samples from store to store, leave literature and order forms, and make follow-up telephone calls. Of course, time spent in selling your toys is time that could be spent in the workshop making them. Many toymakers would rather pay someone else to do the selling for them. It may be possible to convince a sales representative or sales brokerage company to include your toys among the many product lines they sell.

Q. What are the advantages of having a sales representative?
A. Good sales representatives can reach buyers who otherwise would not be available. By enlisting their help you will benefit from the customers, contacts, and reputation that they have already established. Additionally, many sales representatives are affiliated with other sales organizations. This could be important if you ever wish to expand your sales into other territories. Sales representatives work on a commission basis. They are considered independent contractors rather than employees. Consequently, you will avoid the taxation and

bookkeeping complications, as well as the other added expenses of being an employer.

Q. How much would I be expected to pay a sales representative?
A. Details of an agreement between you and a sales company must be worked out individually. Commissions are generally around 15–20% of the wholesale price of the toy. The representative would probably want you to provide sales samples and literature and may charge an extra fee for showing your line of toys at national gift and trade shows.

A written agreement should clearly state the method of compensation. In some cases, the commission will become due as soon as you receive the purchase order. In other cases, you will be allowed to wait until after the toys have been delivered and you have received payment from a store, before paying the commission. The latter is obviously more advantageous from the toymaker's point of view. Besides giving the toymaker more capital to work with for a longer time, it also gives a salesperson reason to be concerned about a company's credit rating. With a vested interest, they are more apt to deal with companies that have a history of prompt payments.

Q. Once I receive an order and ship the merchandise, can I expect to receive payment right away?
A. No. In most cases, you will be asked to sell your toys on credit. Although it is possible to sell toys on a cash-only basis, this is a practice generally reserved for retail sales and will severely limit the number of wholesale orders you receive. It is standard practice to require payment thirty days after the invoice date.

A discount for early payment and a penalty for late payment are often used to speed the flow of cash. Terms of sale should be clearly stated on the order form and invoice. 2%–10/Net 30, for example, tells the purchaser that payment is due 30 days after the date of the invoice, but that if payment is made within 10 days, 2% can be deducted from the bill (excluding shipping charges). The amount that may be charged customers for overdue accounts is regulated by state law. A typical statement of terms would read: "A late fee of 1½% per month, 18% per annum will be charged on past-due accounts."

Q. How do I know what price to set for my toys?
A. Pricing can be a difficult and complex problem. On one hand, you want to recover the money you have invested in making a toy—you want to be paid for your time—and you want to make a profit. On the other hand, your toys must be priced competitively if you expect people to buy them.

To get an accurate idea of where your toys fit into the marketplace, you'll need to compare objectively your toys to those offered by other craftspeople. Note the range of prices, the materials used, the quality of craftsmanship, and the creativity of design. Then you can estimate a fair retail price for your own toys. If you are selling your toys wholesale, your share will be approximately 50% of this price.

You will then need to figure, as accurately as possible, the actual cost of producing the toy. Remember to include your general overhead costs such as electricity, rent, and insurance in the calculation, as well as advertising, packaging, labor, and sales commissions. If you determine that the cost of producing the toy will be more than you could reasonably expect to charge for it, you will need to find a way to cut

your costs or you will have to remove the toy from your line.

Here are some ways that you can cut costs:
——Redesign the toy to be faster to produce.
——Shop for less expensive materials (perhaps buying in larger quantities).
——Make use of time-saving production techniques.
——Decrease operating costs.
Keep in mind that you will encounter less competition with a uniquely designed toy and will then have more freedom to determine its price.

Q. What about consignment?
A. Some retail stores carry inventory on consignment. Under such an agreement, they display your toys, but are under no obligation to buy them. You receive money only after a toy has been sold. Of course, an agreed-upon percentage of the retail selling price is withheld to compensate the store owner. This percentage is usually between 20–40% of the retail price.

Most toymakers would rather sell their toys outright, looking upon consignment as a last resort. After all, it's better to have cash to reinvest, than to have inventory sitting on the store shelf. But it may be necessary to place expensive one-of-a-kind toys on consignment, since retailers might be reluctant to buy these items outright.

Q. What can I offer a store owner that a huge toy manufacturer can't?
A. You will be able to offer toys that are out of the ordinary. Gift shops and mail-order firms look hard to find unusual products. They are in the business of selling special gifts that are not carried by every major store in the country. A unique toy is a salable toy.

You can also offer fast services. By keeping an inventory of toys, you will be able to ship orders immediately. This can be especially important when filling Christmas orders. Store owners are usually required to order Christmas toys months in advance. If they do not accurately project their toy sales, they may end up with little to sell in the final weeks before Christmas. You can take advantage of these sales opportunities by offering immediate shipment or delivery.

Major toy manufacturers require buyers to place large orders and to buy dozens of each toy. You can allow your customers to place smaller orders made up of a variety of toys.

Q. How can I protect my toy from being duplicated by another toymaker?
A. The answer that first comes to mind is to get a patent. Although a patent provides a great deal of protection, acquiring one is not an easy task. The first step is to convince yourself that you've invented a totally new and unique toy. The next step is to hire a patent attorney who will, after a patent search, prepare and submit a detailed application to the U.S. Patent Office. Thousands of dollars and several years later, you may be the proud owner of a U.S. patent. It is more likely, however, that the patent search will turn up a similar toy, or that the patent office will reject your application. If you feel that your idea has the potential to become the next national craze, by all means contact a patent attorney. If not, consider copyrighting your toy, rather than patenting it.

Just as the author of an original literary work is protected by the copyright law, so too is the "author" of an original work of visual art. Unlike the patent, however, the copyright does not protect the construction or mechanics of a toy. It protects only the particular look of a toy and not the basic idea.

Q. How do I go about copyrighting a toy?
A. The present law provides for automatic copyright protection as soon as a work is created. However, in order to make a public record of your copyright, you will need to register it with the Copyright Office in Washington D.C. This is an inexpensive and simple matter that does not require the services of a lawyer. Here's how to go about it:

On the bottom of the very first copy of the toy you have designed and are offering for sale, and on each subsequent copy, mark a notice of copyright. This can be done with a rubber stamp, a branding tool, or with a pen, as long as it is clearly legible. It must include the following three elements:

1. The symbol © (the letter c in a circle)
2. The year the "copies" of the work were first made public.
3. The name of the owner of the copyright.

Take photographs of the toy. These must show the "entire copyrightable content" including the copyright notice. Obtain two prints of each photo and (on the back of these) print the title of your work and the exact measurement of at least one of its dimensions. Send these photographs, along with a completed application form VA and a non-refundable filing fee of $10.00 to the Register of Copyrights in Washington, D.C. (See appendix for more information).

If your application is in proper form and if your work is accepted for registration, you will be mailed a certificate of registration in approximately 120 days. Copyright is a good investment when you consider that your copyright will last 50 years longer than you will. But the best protection is to continuously come up with new and innovative toys to add to your line.

Q. What kind of paperwork do I need to know about?

A. Let's follow the paper trail from the original order to the receipt of payment. First, you will receive an order either written on a store's *purchase order form* or on the *order form* you have provided. This form should include: the terms of sale, the price of each item, the requested date of shipment and the signature of the buyer.

Next, as packages are readied for shipment, a *packing slip* is enclosed. The packing slip should include: the customer's purchase order number (PO#), the number of boxes included in the shipment, and the weight and destination of the packages. When arranging for shipping, the post office or the United Parcel Ser-

vice will provide you with a *receipt*, or in the case of shipment by truck, you will have a copy of the *bill of lading*.

After the toys have been shipped, the buyer will be expecting an itemized bill or *invoice*. It should include the unit price of each toy, the number of units of each toy shipped, the cost of shipping, the terms of sale, and the date.

Then, a monthly *statement* should be sent to inform the buyer of an outstanding balance. It should refer to the invoice number and include all monthly fees charged for late payment.

Finally, a check is received for payment of the shipment. All paperwork should be dated and copies should be kept for your records.

Production Tips

It seemed like a good idea at the time. Instead of laboriously hand-sanding each toy part, why not put them all in a box with some sand and put the box in the clothes dryer? Imagine—sand while you sleep!

The parcel was carefully prepared and placed in the dryer with anticipation. We chose the setting . . . fluff . . . durable press . . . thirty minutes . . . on . . .

CLUNK. KWAK. THUMP. Music to our ears.

We went confidently into the kitchen for lunch, thinking of the time we would save. We couldn't wait to see the results—all the toy pieces effortlessly sanded to perfection.

The unmistakable smell of fried electrical parts interrupted our meal. We ran to the garage and flung open the dryer door. Sand was everywhere. Smoke was everywhere.

The overloaded motor had burned up. The toy parts emerged badly dented from whirling around at too high a speed.

Standing bewildered in a haze of smoke, surveying the disaster surrounding us, we asked the age-old question: "Did Alexander Graham Bell have days like this?"

Eventually, we did come up with a workable plan for a tumble sander and we've included it in this section along with other production tips.

Increasing Production

As the word of your quality wooden toys spreads, you may find yourself hard pressed to keep up with the demand. Since your success in the toy business depends upon your ability to meet this demand, you may need to find ways to increase your production. You might dream of eventually owning a toy factory, complete with automatic lathes, four-sided shapers and a personnel department. But in the meantime, here are some ways to increase production without hiring employees or buying expensive machinery.

ORGANIZE FOR EFFICIENCY

Ask yourself how much time you waste searching through the sawdust to find a pencil, through a box to find a pattern, or through a tool chest to find a drill bit. Chances are, the answer is "too much." Increased production can be as simple as becoming more organized, and a good place to start is with the common sense advice: find a place for everything and put everything back in its place.

Patterns: Once a toy has been designed, make a pattern of each of its pieces. Use a thin durable material such as hardboard or masonite so that the pattern will be easy to draw around and will retain its shape even after hundreds of uses. If you have the wall space, it's a good idea to drill a hole in each pattern piece and to hang it on a peg. Draw around each pattern to reserve its place. If wall space is not available, find some other method of storage which will allow you to retrieve the patterns with ease.

Wood Scraps: Most toymakers find it difficult to throw away scrap wood. They are tempted to save every small piece for use in the future. But as the scrap pile becomes larger and larger, it becomes more and more difficult to store these scraps in an organized fashion. The money saved in using scrap wood is often offset by the time it takes to search through an enormous pile to find the appropriate piece of lumber. You can solve this problem by saving fewer scraps and by organizing the scraps you choose to save.

Wood scraps should be organized according to type of wood, thickness and length. Ideally, the scraps should be stacked on storage shelves. Part of this organization system should include receptacles for the scraps you intend to sell, burn or give away.

Shop Space: Imagine a shop arranged so that the drill press is against one wall and the drill bits are located in a cabinet positioned against the opposite wall. The amount of time wasted in changing drill bits might, at first, seem insignificant. But when you consider the number of times per day that drill bits are changed, and multiply the wasted time by days, weeks and years, it is easy to see that the arrangement of a workshop is extremely important.

Working out an ideal shop arrangement is not easy. Arranging a small work space can be like solving a jigsaw puzzle; only one possible arrangement will allow all the pieces to fit together. With a large work space, the problem can be just the opposite; there are so many possibilities that it is difficult to know where to start.

Whether working with a large or small work space, planning a new shop, or rearranging an old one, it is helpful to make a scale drawing of the floor plan and to use paper cut-outs to test the possible arrangements of tools, machinery, workbenches and storage racks. Here are some factors which should also be considered in your plan:

——Tools, accessories and materials should be located as closely as possible to their areas of use.

——Electrical outlets should be plotted on your floor plan and considered in the layout of your shop.

——Lumber should be stored in an area that is convenient to the access door as well as to the radial arm and/or table saw.

——Workbenches and machinery should be well lit.

Production: Once your work space has been organized, you will want to organize the production process itself.

You don't need to be an expert to know that it is more efficient to make ten biplanes all at one time, than to make ten biplanes one at a time. The time lost in locating and retrieving materials, adjusting tools and walking between work stations would be cut by 90%. This same principle is true for all phases of toy production, including finishing, packaging and shipping. So the first step in organizing production is to plan for the longest feasible run of each toy. When possible, combine orders rather than fill one order at a time. Aim at building an inventory of toys and scheduling regular runs to replenish your stock.

It is often helpful to make a written production plan for each run. This plan should include the number of units you plan to produce, a list of materials you will need to have on hand, a step-by-step sequence of production, and a timetable for completing each task. This type of plan not only helps you to keep on schedule, but will also be helpful when ordering supplies and evaluating the price you charge for each toy.

Part of production planning is scheduling for regular clean-up and maintenance. Plan to clean your shop after every production step. A clean shop is more efficient than a cluttered one. Regular maintenance will result in tools which work faster and break down less often.

USING PRE-MANUFACTURED TOY PARTS

The use of commercially made toy parts is a hot issue with some toymakers. There are those who swear by the use of manufactured wheels and toy parts and others who feel that parts made by automatic machines have no place on "hand-crafted" toys. They could not dispute, however, the fact that premanufactured toy parts significantly reduce the time it takes to make a toy. If you decide to use commercial parts, you will find a number of companies offering a large selection of parts from which to choose.

Turned parts include: wheels, smokestacks, people, pegs, balls, barrels, drums, milk cans, headlights, yo-yos, tops, checkers, game pawns, cribbage pegs, and many others. Parts are available in a variety of woods and colors.

In addition to turned parts, wooden moldings are available. These machined lengths of wood have already been shaped and are ready to be cut to length for use as fenders, cabs and bumpers.

If a company doesn't stock the toy part you need, you might contact a company that makes custom wood shapes. Such companies specialize in manufacturing parts to specification and provide a price quotation after receiving a detailed sketch or sample. The catch is that you will be expected to order a large quantity of each custom-made part (at least 5,000). You will probably be charged a one-time tooling fee in addition to the price per piece. Most toymakers find the expense of custom parts to be prohibitive and choose to either make their own parts or to order standard parts from mail-order catalogues.

TUMBLE SANDER

Let's face it, some toymakers do a better job of sanding their toys than do others. After all, sanding is not the most pleasant way to spend your time. Sanding small toys parts can be especially tedious. Wouldn't it be nice if there were a way to automatically sand small wood toy parts? Here is a machine that is guaranteed to tumble away the sanding blues.

A tumble sander is simply a sturdy barrel, which revolves at a slow speed on a motorized base. Approximately ¼ of the barrel is filled with torn-up pieces of sandpaper. (This is a great way to make use of used abrasive sheets that would ordinarily be thrown away.) The small toy parts are then placed in the barrel. As it turns, the continuous movement smooths the toy parts in much the same way that stones are smoothed in a rock polisher. The longer the parts are allowed to tumble the smoother they become.

A tumble sander is not without limitations. Even though it can cut down on the amount of hand-labor involved in sanding, it cannot eliminate it completely. Some preliminary sanding is still needed. Additionally, you will have better results with tumbling certain toy parts. Here are some of the variables:

——the shape, size and weight of the pieces to be tumbled
——the number of pieces tumbled
——the variety of wood used
——the amount of abrasive used
——the speed of rotation
——the amount of time the parts are allowed to tumble.

Plan: This is the tumble sander that we made to tumble small toy parts (Illus. 116a). We used two rollers, scavenged from an old discarded warehouse conveyer system. These were equipped with internal bearings. Onto one of these rollers, we welded an iron pulley. Since we used a motor which turned at 1750 RPM, but wanted the barrel to revolve very slowly (9-12 RPM), we needed to use a series of pulleys, belts and arbors.

A simpler way to make the tumble sander is to substitute ¾"-dia. shafts for the rollers and to use standard pillow-block bearings. A pulley could then be mounted directly to one shaft without the need for welding. A speed reducer (5:1 gear ratio), could be used to slow the RPM, eliminating the need for so many pulleys and belts.

The barrel is made of wood. Its ends are 22" in diameter and are cut from ¾"-thick plywood. After gluing and nailing 1½"-wide slats to the circumference, we attached rubber strips cut from old tires for traction and cushioning.

TUMBLE SANDER

Ref.	Part	Diameter	Number
A	Roller	1⅞"	2
B	Alignment Bearing	1¼"	2
C	Drive Wheel Pulley	3¾"	1
D	Pulley	3"	1
E	Pulley	2½"	1
F	Motor—¾ HP-1750 RPM		
G	Pulley	2"	1
H	Pulley	10"	1
I	Pulley	7"	1

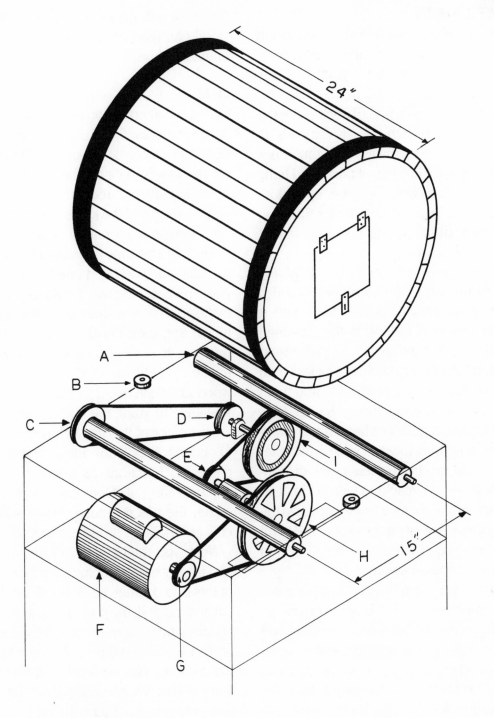

Illus. 134. Tumble sander.

119

AUTOMATIC OILER

There are a number of ways to apply a finish to a toy, but most are time-consuming or impractical. Applying a finish with a paint brush is inefficient. Spraying a finish requires an air compressor, a spray gun, and (if done properly) a paint booth—and much of the finish ends up in the air, rather than on the toy. It is sometimes possible to dip a toy in a can of finish and hang it up to dry, but this can be a messy operation. The quickest and easiest method for finishing toys is to use a natural oil finish (such as walnut oil) in an automatic oiler.

"Oh sure!" you are probably thinking. "Where am I going to get an automatic oiler, and how many thousands of dollars will it cost?" The answer is to look in the classified section of your local newspaper. You are bound to find a number of used machines for less than $100. Oh, by the way, don't expect to find them listed under tools and machinery. Rather, look under the kitchen appliances heading. An automatic oiler is nothing more than a dishwasher which has had the heating elements disconnected. By filling the machine with oil instead of water, and running it for a few seconds on the wash cycle, toys placed on the racks inside will be coated with oil. The excess oil will drip to the bottom to be used again.

But how do you keep the oil from pumping out on the floor by mistake? On some machines it is an easy matter to disconnect the float and to plug the outflow hose into the float receptacle, so that when oil is pumped through this hose, it will enter the machine again for automatic recycling. Another alternative is to simply put the outflow hose in a five-gallon can and to position the can level with the fluid inside. A piece of nylon stocking or net over the end of this hose will filter out impurities. The bucket of oil can then be dumped back into the machine by hand.

JIGS

Many toymakers, upon evaluating their toymaking procedures, find a number of steps that can be made easier or eliminated altogether with the use of jigs. A jig can be any device to assist in the toymaking procedure. The following examples illustrate the kinds of toymaking operations to which jigs can be applied.

First, let's assume that you are making tic-tac-toe sets, and you need one hundred X-shaped game pieces. One way to proceed would be to make an X pattern, draw around it one hundred times, and then cut the pieces out freehand, one at a time, on the bandsaw. A much faster method would be to cut square sections of wood and then use a jig clamped to the bandsaw table to guide the cutting (Illus. 133).

One piece of this jig (A) functions as a fence to accurately position the cut while the other piece (B) functions as a stop to control the depth of the cut. Once the first four cuts are made, the piece is turned over and the final cuts are made to produce the X piece.

Next, you might want to make a number of rocking pig banks (included in the plan section of this book). Once all of the pieces have been cut and sanded, the pigs are ready to assemble. Holding the ends of the pig in the correct position and location while at the same time attaching the slats can be a difficult and time-consuming task. One solution is to enlist on extra pair of hands. Another solution is to make and use a "Pig Jig" (Illus. 134).

This jig will hold the two pieces in perfect alignment, parallel and vertical, while the slats

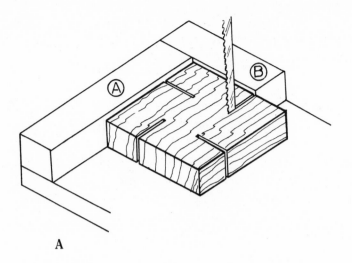

A

Illus. 135. X-jig.

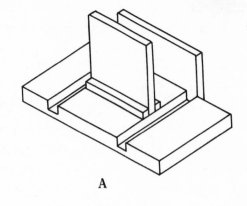

A

Illus. 136. Pigjig.

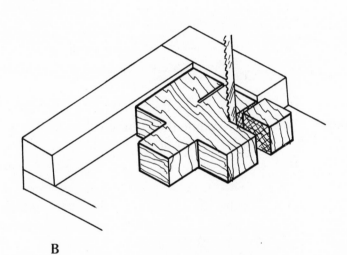

B

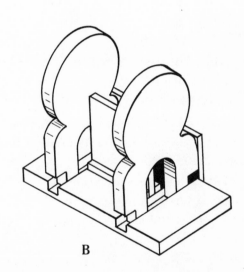

B

Make a habit of evaluating your production procedures often. You may find that a simple jig can make the difference between a profitable toy and one that's not.

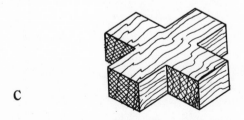

C

are being attached. It will greatly increase your efficiency, and yet, it is essentially a 2 × 12 board with two grooves dadoed into it.

APPENDICES

METRIC EQUIVALENCY CHART

MM—MILLIMETRES   CM—CENTIMETRES

INCHES TO MILLIMETRES AND CENTIMETRES

INCHES	MM	CM	INCHES	CM	INCHES	CM
⅛	3	0.3	9	22.9	30	76.2
¼	6	0.6	10	25.4	31	78.7
⅜	10	1.0	11	27.9	32	81.3
½	13	1.3	12	30.5	33	83.8
⅝	16	1.6	13	33.0	34	86.4
¾	19	1.9	14	35.6	35	88.9
⅞	22	2.2	15	38.1	36	91.4
1	25	2.5	16	40.6	37	94.0
1¼	32	3.2	17	43.2	38	96.5
1½	38	3.8	18	45.7	39	99.1
1¾	44	4.4	19	48.3	40	101.6
2	51	5.1	20	50.8	41	104.1
2½	64	6.4	21	53.3	42	106.7
3	76	7.6	22	55.9	43	109.2
3½	89	8.9	23	58.4	44	111.8
4	102	10.2	24	61.0	45	114.3
4½	114	11.4	25	63.5	46	116.8
5	127	12.7	26	66.0	47	119.4
6	152	15.2	27	68.6	48	121.9
7	178	17.8	28	71.1	49	124.5
8	203	20.3	29	73.7	50	127.0

YARDS TO METRES

YARDS	METRES	YARDS	METRES	YARDS	METRES	YARDS	METRES	YARDS	METRES
⅛	0.11	2⅛	1.94	4⅛	3.77	6⅛	5.60	8⅛	7.43
¼	0.23	2¼	2.06	4¼	3.89	6¼	5.72	8¼	7.54
⅜	0.34	2⅜	2.17	4⅜	4.00	6⅜	5.83	8⅜	7.66
½	0.46	2½	2.29	4½	4.11	6½	5.94	8½	7.77
⅝	0.57	2⅝	2.40	4⅝	4.23	6⅝	6.06	8⅝	7.89
¾	0.69	2¾	2.51	4¾	4.34	6¾	6.17	8¾	8.00
⅞	0.80	2⅞	2.63	4⅞	4.46	6⅞	6.29	8⅞	8.12
1	0.91	3	2.74	5	4.57	7	6.40	9	8.23
1⅛	1.03	3⅛	2.86	5⅛	4.69	7⅛	6.52	9⅛	8.34
1¼	1.14	3¼	2.97	5¼	4.80	7¼	6.63	9¼	8.46
1⅜	1.26	3⅜	3.09	5⅜	4.91	7⅜	6.74	9⅜	8.57
1½	1.37	3½	3.20	5½	5.03	7½	6.86	9½	8.69
1⅝	1.49	3⅝	3.31	5⅝	5.14	7⅝	6.97	9⅝	8.80
1¾	1.60	3¾	3.43	5¾	5.26	7¾	7.09	9¾	8.92
1⅞	1.71	3⅞	3.54	5⅞	5.37	7⅞	7.20	9⅞	9.03
2	1.83	4	3.66	6	5.49	8	7.32	10	9.14

Toy Safety

CONSUMER PRODUCTS SAFETY COMMISSION
Washington, D.C.
20207

Regional Office Addresses:

MIDWESTERN REGIONAL OFFICE
230 South Dearborn Street, Rm. 2944
Chicago, IL
60604

SOUTHEASTERN REGIONAL OFFICE
800 Peachtree Street, N.E., Suite 210
Atlanta, GA
30308

SOUTHWESTERN REGIONAL OFFICE
1100 Commerce Street, Rm. 1C10
Dallas, TX
75242

WESTERN REGIONAL OFFICE
555 Battery Street, Rm. 415
San Francisco, CA
94111

NORTHEASTERN REGIONAL OFFICE
6 World Trade Center
Vesey Street, 6th Floor
New York, NY
10048

If you are making toys for resale, you should write to CPSC for a copy of the *Code of Federal Regulations*.

TOY MANUFACTURERS OF AMERICA
200 Fifth Avenue
New York, NY
10010

For information on the Voluntary Standards for Toy Safety (ASTM F 963) contact:

THE AMERICAN SOCIETY FOR TESTING AND MATERIALS
1916 Race Street
Philadelphia, PA
19103

Copyright

To register copyright, send filing fee, copyright form, and required materials for deposit to:

COPYRIGHT OFFICE
Library of Congress
Washington, D.C. 20559

For publications, call the Forms and Publications Hotline, 202-287-9100, or write:

COPYRIGHT OFFICE
Publications Section, LM-455
Library of Congress
Washington, D.C. 20559

To speak with an information specialist or to request further information, call 202-479-0700, or write:

COPYRIGHT OFFICE
Information Section, LM-401
Library of Congress
Washington, D.C. 20559

Illus. 137. Toy parts shown on first page of color section.

Key is as follows:

A	wood balls	H	decorative plugs and buttons
B	wheels	I	wood top
C	smoke stacks	J	headlight
D	people turnings	K	barrels
E	spoked wheel	L	fender moulding
F	hearts	M	game pieces
G	multi-use pegs	N	flat-cut wheel

Index

A
assembly, 23–24*illus.*
automatic oiler, 120

B
baby rattles, 22
bank(s)
    gas pump, 84–90*illus.*
    rocking-pig, 58–62*illus.*
big horn pull toy, 80–83*illus.*
big train, 96–108*illus.*
bill of lading, 114
burning and branding, 27–29*illus.*
buzz saw, 41–44*illus.*

C
caboose, train, 105–107*illus.*
camera, 63–66*illus.*
coal car, 102–104*illus.*
commercial toyselling, 112–114
consignment, 112
copyrighting, 113, 126
cradle, 49–51*illus.*

D
designing toys, 6–7
dimensions, 7, 9–10
Don Quixote, 45–48*illus.*
duck pull toy, 52–54*illus.*
dump truck, 76–79*illus.*

E
edges, rounding of, 24–25*illus.*
engine for train, 96–101*illus.*

F
fasteners, 24
finishes, clear, 19–20

G
gas pump bank, 84–90*illus.*
glue, 23

H
hand tools, 12, 14*illus.*, 16*illus.*
hardwoods, 8–10

I
ideas for toys, 6–7
increasing production, 115–121*illus.*
iron set, 70–72*illus.*

J
jalopy, 73–75*illus.*

L
layout, pattern, 23*illus.*
lumber, 8–10

M
metric equivalency, 124

O
oiler, automatic, 120
oils, natural, 20

P
packing slip, 114
parents, toy safety and, 22
parts, pre-manufactured, 117
patents, 113
patterns, 23*illus.*, 115–116
payment for toys, 111–112
pig jig, 120, 121*illus.*
planer, 16*illus.*
plans for toys, 33, *see also* specific toys
pre-manufactured toy parts, 117
pricing of toys, 112
production tips, 115–121*illus.*
pull toys
    big horn, 80–83*illus.*
    Don Quixote, 45–48*illus.*
    duck, 52–54*illus.*
purchase order form, 114

R
rattles, baby, 22
robot, 91–95*illus.*
rocking-pig bank, 58–62*illus.*

S
safety, 125
    burning and branding, 27–29*illus.*
    durability, 22–24
    finishes, 19–22
    regulations, 21–22
    rounding edges, 24–25*illus.*
    sanding, 25–27*illus.*
    wheelmaking, 30–32*illus.*
sanding, 25–27*illus.*
selling toys, 110–114
sewing machine, 39–40*illus.*
small parts, 21, 26
soft woods, 8–10
statement, 114

T
telephone, 55–57*illus.*
terms of sale, 111–112
toaster, 67–69*illus.*
tools, 11–18*illus.*
train, big, 96–108*illus.*
Trojan Horse, 34–36*illus.*
tumble sander, 117–119*illus.*

W
wheelmaking, 30–32*illus.*
wood(s), 8–10